RECONNECT

What Parents, Psychologists, and Educators are saying about *ReConnect*

Neck bent, eyes locked on a phone, no response—sound familiar? In today's attention economy, nurturing healthy parent/child relationships is a constant challenge. Tieger and Shelby reveal how viewing family dynamics through a personality lens can foster the human connection we all need now more than ever.

Rebekah Seaton, M.Ed.
Early Childhood Educator and Former Chair of Community of Concern, a middle- and high-school parent group focused on adolescent mental health and wellness in CT.

As a person who's been immersed in the world of personality type for more than twenty-fiveyears, the parent of a 17-year-old son (ENTP) and 15-year-old daughter (ESTP), and someone who's acutely aware of the negative impact of digital technology on children, *ReConnect* comes along at exactly the right time! It offers an antidote to the disconnection so many families are experiencing by showing parents how to build healthy, trusting relationships with their kids—including the full range of different personalities!

Rob Toomey, *President of TypeCoach*

As a public-school counselor for 15 years and assistant principal for 8 years, I have witnessed the explosion of digital addiction and how it has significantly diminished children's ability to focus and acquire a comprehensive education. I'm equally concerned at how it has impacted students' ability to communicate and develop healthy relationships with their peers. But I am encouraged by the personalized strategies provided by *ReConnect* and believe they can help parents, children, and educators as they grapple with the challenges posed by widespread digital addiction.

Keats Jarmon, MS
Guidance and Counseling, Sixth Year in Education Leadership

Shows parents how to create a healthier, more meaningful relationship with their child.

Grace Grinnell, *CIT instructor for The CT Alliance to Benefit Law Enforcement (Mental Health Training for First Responders) and parent*

After more than twenty-five years as an educator and as a parent of two teenagers, I've seen firsthand the undeniable link between rising anxiety, depression, and our increasing digital connectivity. This book offers both the evidence and the practical solutions families need to re-engage with one another. This is a must-read so that we can reconnect, redefine, and rebuild our relationships with our children—for the sake of our collective mental health.

Lindsay Tringali, MS
Educational Leadership and Sixth Year in Leadership

We live in trying times of the exponential growth of technology, which has both positive and negative effects on our lives and those of our children. Technical addictions have increased dramatically, especially with children and adolescents, leading to social isolation and increased anxiety. Many children today have difficulty separating fact from fiction and have a lack of empathy and patience. They've lost their sense of wonder.

Despite the challenges to professionals and parents, Shelby and Tieger offer hope and a specific methodology to raise resilient and mentally healthy children in their new book, *ReConnect*. I highly recommend this book to both providers and parents.

Sondra Kronick Frowine, LMFT, LADC

I encourage providers of addiction services to read this book for a helpful overview of the intersection of personality/mental health and technology overuse/addiction to help guide individuals and families in discussing rational approaches to healing and practical change.

Vincent J. McClain, MD,
Program Director, Addiction Medicine Fellowship at Rushford

Over my many years as a high school counselor, I've observed a noticeable increase in the amount of time students spend online. For teens who aren't involved in sports or extracurricular activities, online gaming and social media often become their primary social outlet. While this can provide a sense of connection, it can also lead to increased feelings of isolation in face-to-face social situations. In contrast, students who participate in after-school sports or other structured activities tend to develop stronger social skills, manage their time more effectively, and often maintain a more positive outlook on life. I believe that *ReConnect* can help educators and school counselors better understand and engage with individual students.

Sheila Nussbaum, M.A
Guidance and Counseling, School Counselor

By combining their respective areas of expertise - Tieger's: personality, and Shelby's: treating digital addiction - the authors have created a unique framework that helps parents and therapists collaborate to better understand the child's potential mental health vulnerabilities and customize treatment to be effective with very different types of children. Highly recommended.

Joel Lavenson LPC, LCPC

ReConnect presents solid, scientific evidence that an individual's innate personality type may be an important yet unappreciated risk factor. Helping parents determine if their child may be at increased risk for depression and/or anxiety allows them to seek treatment sooner, which can have a huge impact on the child's mental health.

Maureen McBride, *Parent, Board Member of NAMI Southwest CT, Facilitator of Family Support Group, Youth/Young Adult Mental Health Advocate*

ReConnect © 2025 by Paul Tieger and Michael Shelby

All rights reserved. Printed in the United States of America. No part of this book may be used or reproduced in any manner without the written permission of the author and/or publisher. The only exception to this will be for the use of brief excerpts in critical articles and reviews.

First electronic and bound edition published 2025

ISBN-13: 979-8-9996077-0-6 (print)
ISBN-10: 979-8-9996077-1-3 (e-book)

All trademarks are the property of their respective owners.

Published by Adolescent Mental Health Institute, LLC

Cover Design by Kim Glooch
Book Illustrations by Kim Glooch

Book Design by David Robbins   Typeface: Palatino 11/14
Edited by Jennifer LaRue

23456

RECONNECT

A personalized plan to protect your child from anxiety and depression fueled by digital addiction.

By Paul Tieger, MS and Michael Shelby, LPC

DEDICATIONS

This book is dedicated to parents and family members of everyone whose loved ones are struggling with mental-health challenges and communication.

Anxiety, depression, and addiction come in many forms.

Kind, open, and clear communication is always the first step toward recovery.

To all those who came before me, and took that step and showed me the way out.

I dedicate this book to you…

Michael Shelby

To Herbie, Evelyn, Marc, Kelly, Danny, Barbara, Will, Arlo, Calvin, June, Chris and Emily, who have given me so very much to be grateful for.

Paul Tieger

TABLE OF CONTENTS

18	**Preface**
21	**Chapter 1:** Introduction: What you need to know about *ReConnect*
27	**Chapter 2:** The Real Cost of Digital Technology: The 20 Greatest Dangers of Digital Addiction and One Existential Crisis
43	**Chapter 3:** Personality Type: Why we are who we are
50	**Chapter 4:** Who am I? Who are you? Who are we? Identifying your and your child's personality types

Parent/Child Personality Type Profiles

Responsible Hard Worker Parent

60	**Chapter 5:** Responsible Hard Worker Parent & Child
65	**Chapter 6:** Responsible Hard Worker Parent & Strategic Problem Solver Child
71	**Chapter 7:** Responsible Hard Worker Parent & Adventurous Free Spirit Child
77	**Chapter 8:** Responsible Hard Worker Parent & Gentle Humble Helper Child
83	**Chapter 9:** Responsible Hard Worker Parent & Creative Sensitive Soul Child

Strategic Problem Solver Parent

90	**Chapter 10:** Strategic Problem Solver Parent & Responsible Hard Worker Child
96	**Chapter 11:** Strategic Problem Solver Parent & Child
102	**Chapter 12:** Strategic Problem Solver Parent & Adventurous Free Spirit Child
108	**Chapter 13:** Strategic Problem Solver Parent & Gentle Humble Helper Child
114	**Chapter 14:** Strategic Problem Solver Parent & Creative Sensitive Soul Child

Adventurous Free Spirit Parent

121	**Chapter 15:** Adventurous Free Spirit Parent & Responsible Hard Worker Child
128	**Chapter 16:** Adventurous Free Spirit Parent & Strategic Problem Solver Child
134	**Chapter 17:** Adventurous Free Spirit Parent & Child
140	**Chapter 18:** Adventurous Free Spirit Parent & Gentle Humble Helper Child
146	**Chapter 19:** Adventurous Free Spirit Parent & Creative Sensitive Soul Child

Gentle Humble Helper Parent

154	**Chapter 20:** Gentle Humble Helper Parent & Responsible Hard Worker Child
160	**Chapter 21:** Gentle Humble Helper Parent & Strategic Problem Solver Child
166	**Chapter 22:** Gentle Humble Helper Parent & Adventurous Free Spirit Child
172	**Chapter 23:** Gentle Humble Helper Parent & Child
178	**Chapter 24:** Gentle Humble Helper Parent & Creative Sensitive Soul Child

Creative Sensitive Soul Parent

185	**Chapter 25:** Creative Sensitive Soul Parent & Responsible Hard Worker Child
191	**Chapter 26:** Creative Sensitive Soul Parent & Strategic Problem Solver Child
197	**Chapter 27:** Creative Sensitive Soul Parent & Adventurous Free Spirit Child
203	**Chapter 28:** Creative Sensitive Soul Parent & Gentle Humble Helper Child
210	**Chapter 29:** Creative Sensitive Soul Parent & Child
217	**Chapter 30:** A Vision for You: Final Thoughts, and a Reason to Be Hopeful
222	**Personality Type Resources**
224	**Notes**
226	**Glossary**
228	**Valuable Resources**
234	**Appendix: Additional Data**

ACKNOWLEDGEMENTS

I have to start by thanking my incredible wife, Sabina. From supporting my early incursion into the field of technology addiction and mental health counseling to putting up with long nights of research and writing. Thank you for giving me this space to grow, to learn, and to stay curious. Thank you so much, Sabi!

I also want to thank my friend and my mentor, the late Dr. David Greenfield, for taking a chance and meeting with a complete stranger in the early 2000s. A journey of a thousand miles begins with a single step. Our meeting led me on this incredible journey of more than two decades that changed the course of my life. Thank you for teaching me what cannot be learned from books. I am grateful to you for your guidance, your friendship, your support, and your pioneering spirit in the field of technology addiction.

Finally, I want to thank my co-author Paul Tieger for inspiring me on the spot to jump in with both feet to create this life-saving manual. Thank you for your support and your dedication. This book would never have happened without you.

Michael Shelby, LPC

This book has been forty-five years in the making. It would not have been possible without the wisdom, guidance, and very patient support of countless family members and friends (you know who you are!) who—most often involuntarily—accompanied me on my decades-long study of personality psychology. Most significant among them is my co-author of multiple books, Barbara Barron.

I want to express my very deep gratitude to my mentor and friend Jon Schommer, who recognized how central personality type is to understanding human behavior and invited me to collaborate on several groundbreaking studies, including the research upon which this book is based. Thank you also to Tony Olson and Nate Rickles for your invaluable contributions to this research.

Without the generosity of so many dedicated professionals in the mental-health and suicide-prevention communities, it would have been nearly impossible to create this new framework and tool for helping parents better understand and connect with their children. I'm especially indebted to Dan Weiner, Andrea Duarte, Ann Dagle, Liz Taylor, Grace Grinnell, Rebekah Seaton, Tracy Johnston, Julie Rivnak-McAdam, and Ronnie Walker. My heartfelt appreciation to Lauren Walters for his keen mind, always thought-provoking conversations, creative yet practical suggestions, and unwavering support for many years.

Finally, I'm blessed to have Kim Glooch, Jennifer LaRue, Dave Robbins, and Don Martinez enthusiastically share their sizable talent to make this book a reality. But most of all, I'm indebted to my extraordinary co-author Michael Shelby for agreeing to collaborate with me on this project, which would never have happened had we not been introduced by our mutual friend Richard Sugarman.

Paul Tieger, MS

PREFACE

In today's fast-paced digital world, few issues are as urgent—and as universally misunderstood—as the epidemic of anxiety and depression plaguing our youngest and most vulnerable.

It is an epidemic with ties to digital addiction, ubiquitous screens, and 24/7 connectivity. It was an epidemic exposed and exacerbated by COVID isolation. We are witnessing an explosion of anxiety and depression, not only among children and teens but also among their parents. Entire families now navigate their days isolated, tethered to screens, often unaware of the toll this takes on mental health, relationships, communication, and self-worth. Parents and children are simply talking to each other in different languages—when they talk at all. Despite mounting evidence of the emotional and psychological consequences, a practical, accessible, and personalized approach to understanding and addressing this crisis has been missing—until now.

This groundbreaking book is the result of a unique collaboration between two leading experts in their fields: Paul D. Tieger and Michael Shelby. Their partnership brings together decades of insight from two distinct but deeply interconnected worlds—personality psychology and technology addiction treatment.

Paul D. Tieger, MS is an internationally recognized expert in personality type, best known as the co-author of the bestselling books Do What You Are, Nurture by Nature, The Art of SpeedReading People, and Just Your Type. His books have sold more than one million copies and have been translated into more than a dozen languages. For more than 40 years, Paul has helped individuals, couples, educators, and organizations better understand themselves and others by using unique personality types to bridge communication gaps and build connections.

Most significantly, Paul has conducted game-changing peer-reviewed research, the first to establish a strong linkage between personality type, anxiety, depression, and several other health risk factors.

Michael Shelby, LPC is the founder of the Technology Addiction Center (TAC), a groundbreaking organization that has helped countless individuals and families break free from the grip of digital dependency. With a professional background spanning decades in addiction treatment, Michael brings a rare depth of understanding to the psychological and neurological mechanisms behind screen overuse. His book Technology Addiction: A Guide to Recognize and Deal With Technology Addiction in Our Lives is a powerful resource for those seeking to understand and heal from the consequences of digital overexposure.

What makes this book truly different—and urgently needed—is its synthesis of these two expert domains. This is not another warning about screen time, nor a generic parenting manual. This is the first book that not only explores the causes and consequences of this mental-health crisis in both children and adults but also educates and empowers parents to understand and respond to their children based on their individual personality types.

By learning to speak their children's language, parents can connect more effectively, set healthier boundaries, and help guide their children toward a balanced relationship with technology, with peers, and with other family members. Through real-world case studies, practical tools, and personalized strategies, readers will discover how to tailor conversations, interventions, and expectations to fit the unique psychological needs of each child.

This book stands alone in its ability to offer both insight and action. It is a lifeline for families searching for a way forward in a world where constant connectivity often means constant disconnection from what matters most. With clarity, compassion, and credibility, Paul Tieger and Michael Shelby offer hope—and a roadmap—for a more mindful, healthy, and connected future.

Welcome to the first truly personalized guide to navigating today's complex family dynamics and healing from anxiety, depression, and digital addiction.

CHAPTER 1

Introduction

What you need to know about ReConnect

In considering how to best introduce this book, we asked ourselves what would be most helpful for parents to know? Here's what we came up with.

Who are you guys, and what makes you qualified to write this book?
Paul
    For as long as I can remember, I've been fascinated with understanding what makes people tick. My curiosity grew into an obsession when I learned about Carl Jung's personality type theory. Early on, I was fortunate enough to be mentored by the giants in the field of personality psychology, including a major collaborator of Isabel Myers, creator of the Myers-Briggs Type Indicator® (MBTI®)—the world's most respected personality assessment.

    Over the next forty-five years, I co-authored several breakthrough books with Barbara Barron. Do What You Are, the first book to link inborn personality type with career choice, satisfaction, and success, became a monster bestseller, selling more than 1 million copies in six editions. It was followed by Nurture by Nature, The Art of SpeedReading People, and Just Your Type.

    For thirty-five years I was a jury consultant, helping trial attorneys select and influence jurors in high-profile civil and criminal cases, the most famous being the first physician-assisted suicide trial of Dr. Jack Kevorkian.

    But I realized that I had a more important contribution to make when I was invited to collaborate with researchers at the University of Minnesota College of Pharmacy. We conducted five first-of-their-kind peer-reviewed studies, all with large, representative samples. The results revealed that certain individuals' inborn personality types predisposed them to anxiety, depression, alcohol overuse, smoking, sleep issues, and medication non-adherence.

This career-culminating research led me to find my calling: to apply what I've learned over forty-five years to save children and adolescents the anguish of suffering from anxiety and depression.

Okay, Michael. Your turn.

Michael

I am a therapist who specializes in treating adolescents for digital addiction. This experience, combined with my work as an author and educator, makes me uniquely qualified to write about the epidemic of anxiety and depression in children and adolescents, particularly as it relates to digital technology and social media use.

ReConnect addresses how critical developmental processes, such as active, first-hand experiential learning, are being replaced by passive, screen-based content consumption. This shift can have a significant impact on young people's mental well-being.

My expertise in treating adolescents struggling with digital addiction provides a deep understanding of the challenges they face and the specific ways technology use can contribute to increased anxiety and depression. I also understand the importance of parents' building trusting relationships with their children, especially those at increased risk due to their personality types. This book offers parents the insights and personalized advice they need to connect with their children and protect them in our increasingly digital world.

Why is digital technology, and especially digital addiction, such a huge problem?

Paul

In ReConnect we look at digital addiction both from the macro perspective, which describes the enormous scope and consequences of this problem, and from the micro perspective, how it affects individuals and what kind of treatment can be most helpful. I'm the macro guy. I won't pull any punches. I consider addiction to digital technology to be the most pernicious of all addictions— and an existential threat to the human species. Sound hyperbolic? Consider this: relatively few people drink alcohol, take drugs, gamble, smoke, eat, or have sex all day long. But as many as five billion people on the planet don't feel they can function without their electronic devices.

Michael

I feel that Paul is absolutely right. Growing obsession with technology, especially social media, has become one of the quietest yet most dangerous forces shaping our lives. It's not just about spending too much time online; it's about what we're losing in the process—our presence, our peace, our connection to one another. Think about it: billions of people around the world now feel anxious or incomplete without their phones in hand. And while adults struggle, too, it's our kids who are paying the highest price. Their imaginations, confidence, and sense of self are being shaped by screens instead of real experiences. When children stop exploring, building, and feeling the world around them, a vital part of their growth fades. That's why, more than ever, we need to look up, reach out, and reconnect—not through Wi-Fi signals, but through eye contact, laughter, and love.

This book links personality type with depression and anxiety.
Is there any scientific evidence to back that up?

Paul

Yes. And it's compelling. A brief description is provided in Chapter 2, and access to the entire body of published research is provided in the back of the book.

Michael

Our experiences complement one another perfectly. Paul's quantitative studies provide solid scientific evidence, while my twenty years of clinical experience offer complementary insight. My understanding is both scientific and empirical (derived from my practice), linking personality type with depression and anxiety. It aligns with a growing body of research exploring the interplay between our innate personality traits and our mental well-being. It makes a lot of sense that certain personality types might be more predisposed to experiencing anxiety and depression, especially in today's digitally saturated world.

As more and more parents become concerned, several books have been written about this topic. How is your book different?

Paul

First, we need to recognize the tremendous contribution psychologist Jonathan Haidt has made in publishing his ground-breaking book The Anxious Generation, which I consider to be 100% complementary with ReConnect.

The Anxious Generation, which made the world aware of the causes and great harm posed by digital technology and addiction, has had a huge impact not only in the United States but around the world. And while it does provide parents with some generic advice, it doesn't offer parents advice on how to help their specific child. ReConnect takes a very different approach: the entire book is devoted to helping parents understand THEIR child's potential vulnerabilities and offers concrete targeted advice as to how to best protect that child.

Clearly ReConnect *is different, but what makes you think it will work?*

Michael

We believe it can make a huge difference if parents themselves leave their own digital bubble and invest their time interacting with their children in the real world. Without screens. Talking to their children based on the personality type of each child. Based on my experience, personal face-to-face communication is the basis of building trust, and trust is a key component in building a successful, long-lasting, and deep relationship between the child and parent. Our book helps parents learn to speak the language their children can understand, based on their individual type.

Paul

Having thought about, researched, written, and lectured about personality psychology for forty-five years, I've seen countless examples of how understanding one's own, and one's child's, personality type can be life changing. Most pertinent to this work was my second book Nurture by Nature. Co-authored by Barbara Barron, it was the first book to provide parents with new insights about their child based on personality type. Through the years we've heard innumerable parents express a similar sentiment: "I don't know where this child came from! S/he's so different from me, my spouse, and our other children." But we've been extremely gratified when these parents share that they now "get" their child and report that the specific strategies they learned from Nurture by Nature have greatly improved their relationship with their child and positively affected their families.

So, yes. I do believe that ReConnect can help build happier, healthier families, and I am eager to hear from parents for whom it has.

Who is ReConnect for? And how can they get the most out of this book?

Paul and Michael

We believe that ReConnect can be extremely helpful for parents, children, families, and the people who support them, including grandparents, pediatricians, school counselors, psychologists, and other care givers.

We've organized *ReConnect* to make the material as clear and useful as possible. The book begins with psychologist Michael Shelby providing a solid understanding of addiction and depression and how digital addiction increases the risk of both to children. Next, personality expert Paul Tieger introduces the Jung/Myers model of personality type and provides a validated assessment to help you identify your and your child's personality type. Then you will be directed to the chapter exclusively about you and your child, which reveals how your personality-type similarities and differences affect your relationship and offers proven strategies for how to best engage and nurture your child.

ReConnect concludes with a list and description of valuable resources.

Before you jump into the solution, here is a quick test to tell you whether there is a problem that requires solving. Take the following short quiz before peeking at the scoring.

Digital Addiction Quiz

Do you find yourself, your co-parent, or your child:

	PARENT 1	PARENT 2	CHILD
1. Spending more and more time online or on the digital devices (computer, phone, tablet) than you or your child seem to realize, even forgetting homework and chores?			
2. Immediately and almost instinctively reaching down and looking at the phone at every opportunity (waiting in line, at the traffic light, in the bathroom)?			
3. Spending more time with "virtual friends" via online games and social media as opposed to real people nearby and preferring to text rather than talk?			
4. Sleeping with the smartphone powered on under the pillow or next to the bed?			
5. Viewing and answering texts, tweets, and emails at all hours of the day and night, even during family meals, outings, and other events?			
6. Experiencing a decline in academic or work-place productivity, time spent reading books or socializing in person, participating in family or physical activities?			
7. Feeling ill-at-ease, uncomfortable, disconnected, or anxious when accidentally leaving a smartphone in the car or at home, when there is no service, or if the device is broken?			
8. Feeling "normal" only when connected, and otherwise feeling restless?			
9. Having a very strong emotional or even physical reaction to the threat of having the smartphone taken away (as a punishment or otherwise) and constantly arguing about screen time, even with yourself?			
10. Reaching for the smartphone first thing upon awakening?			

Scoring:

If 3 or more boxes are checked under a single person, it is likely that that individual's digital device use is problematic, indicating some form of digital addiction.

CHAPTER 2
The Real Cost of Digital Technology
The 20 Greatest Dangers of Digital Addiction and One Existential Crisis

Once upon a time, patience was a virtue, hard work was admired, and "you get what you pay for" was a commonly accepted truth. But about twenty-five years ago, as society shifted from analog to digital technology, our values shifted, too. Now what we prize most is convenience—easy, instant, and free.

At first glance, this seems harmless, even beneficial. But as with the parable of the boiling frog, danger comes not from sudden shocks but from slow, unnoticed change. A frog dropped into boiling water jumps out immediately. But a frog placed in cool water that is slowly heated won't notice until it's too late. In the same way, our gradual dependence on digital technology has become an existential threat, quietly reshaping human behavior, relationships, and mental health.

The facts are sobering. The average American checks their phone more than 200 times a day, spending about 5 hours daily staring at a screen. More than 81% check their phones within 10 minutes of waking up. Nearly half (48%) of internet users say they feel "addicted" or "somewhat addicted" to their devices— many experts believe this is a serious underestimate. And this isn't just a youth problem: 79% of people over age 65 own smartphones, and many are just as tethered to them as their grandchildren are.

Unlike alcohol or drugs, the delivery system for digital addiction is always within reach, 24/7, in your pocket, on your nightstand, or even strapped to your wrist. Unlike cigarettes, which were eventually banned from being advertised, Big Tech spends more than $200 billion a year marketing digital products. The average person has about 40 apps on their phone.

Major Depression Among Teens

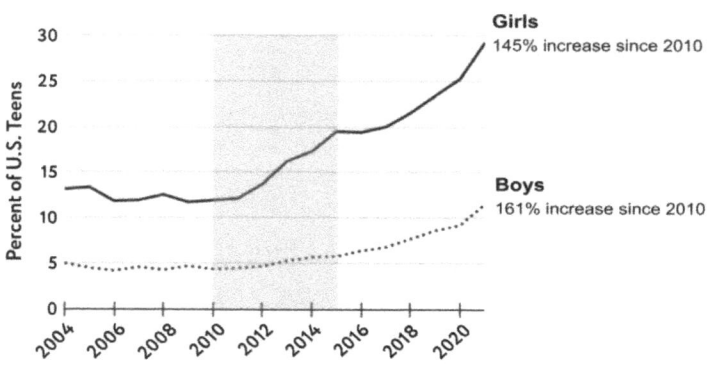

Figure 1.1. Percent of U.S. teens (ages 12–17) who had at least one major depressive episode in the past year, by self-report based on a symptom checklist. This was figure 7.1 in *The Coddling of the American Mind*, now updated with data beyond 2016. (Source: U.S. National Survey on Drug Use and Health.)[3]

The SAMSHA data is clear - since 2012, when smartphones and social media went mainstream, rates of anxiety and depression among adolescents have soared. Nearly 1 in 9 children ages 3–17 has diagnosed anxiety, and 1 in 12 has a diagnosed behavior disorder. Our overdependence on screens is eroding essential human qualities—and hitting children hard.

Below, we outline what we see as the 20 most harmful consequences of digital addiction. Each one chips away at the skills, strengths, and connections children, and families, need to thrive.

I. Knowledge Without Understanding

We live in an age in which almost any question can be answered instantly. Google's own internal reports that the company makes public now show that the company processes more than 8.5 billion searches every day, and the average person conducts about four searches daily. With artificial intelligence generating many of those responses, the process has become even more immediate. But while instant access provides convenience, it doesn't lead to deep understanding.

When we rely on devices to supply answers, we confuse information with knowledge. True knowledge is built through reflection, practice, and integration of ideas into our lived experience. Without this process, our children risk growing up knowing a little about everything but understanding almost nothing.

Example: A 13-year-old boy proudly rattled off facts about black holes he had read online. But when asked why black holes matter to scientists, he fell silent. He could recite trivia, but not meaning. His parents justifiably worried he was learning "bits and bytes" but not how to think deeply.

2. Outsourcing Our Memory

Memory is like a muscle: it grows stronger with use. But when we rely on devices to remember birthdays, phone numbers, directions, and even our grocery lists, we deprive our brains of vital exercise. Shana K. Carpenter's research in Nature Reviews Psychology shows that memorization strengthens neural pathways, supports focus, and builds resilience in problem-solving. By outsourcing everything to devices, we risk cognitive atrophy.

GPS is a prime example. Few people today can navigate their own neighborhood without it. Health apps count our steps, monitor our sleep, and even tell us when to hydrate, skills humans once relied on their senses to track. Convenience comes at a cost; we weaken our ability to recall information and lose confidence in our natural judgment.

Example: A high school girl panicked when her phone battery died. She couldn't remember her best friend's phone number, though they texted daily. For her, memory had been outsourced entirely to the device.

3. Struggling to Tell Fact from Fiction

Our children are growing up in a world saturated with misinformation, even before AI-generated content, fake news, doctored photos, and misleading headlines were rampant. Now, distinguishing truth from fabrication is harder than ever. Both Gallup and Pew Research show that 39% of Americans express "no trust at all" in news media, and confidence in government is even lower, with only 23% saying they trust federal institutions to do what's right.

This erosion of trust leaves kids vulnerable to manipulation. Adolescents, with their developing critical thinking skills, are especially at risk of believing whatever appears most often in their feed. When algorithms feed them biased or misleading content, they lack the tools to push back.

Example: A father described how his 15-year-old daughter became convinced of a conspiracy theory she saw on TikTok. "Everyone online says it," she argued, dismissing her dad's attempts to show her the truth. For her, repetition equaled reality.

4. Confusing Relationships with Technology

When children say they "love" their iPhone, or that Alexa "understands them," it may sound cute, but it's also a red flag. Emotional language meant for human connection is increasingly applied to machines. Tech companies deliberately encourage this, giving devices human names like Siri or Alexa, designing them to respond in warm, helpful voices.

For adolescents still developing social and emotional intelligence, this blurs the boundary between genuine intimacy and functional utility. If kids begin to equate emotional connection with the instant responsiveness of technology, real-world relationships—messy, unpredictable, and requiring patience—may feel frustrating or unrewarding by comparison.

Example: A 12-year-old boy told his parents he "loved" his gaming console more than anything. They laughed, but his mom admitted later she wasn't sure he was joking.

5. Numbed Empathy

Humans are wired to feel compassion for those around us. But digital technology exposes us to suffering on a global scale—famine, wars, disasters—every time we open a feed. Psychologists call it "compassion fatigue." Our brains simply weren't designed to process tragedy at this volume. To cope, many kids (and adults) numb themselves.

The result: desensitization. Teens scroll past painful images without flinching. Over time, this reduced empathy spills into their personal lives. If they can tune out strangers' suffering so easily, they may become less attuned to the struggles of friends, siblings, or parents.

Kids who spend a lot of time playing violent video games can start to become numb to things like death and destruction. The American Psychological Association points out that repeated exposure to violent games is linked to less empathy and more aggressive attitudes in children (APA, 2020). One study even found that just 40 minutes of violent gameplay was enough to lower kids' natural empathic response when seeing someone else in pain (Krahé et al., 2011, Psychophysiology). Other research shows that kids who play these games often may not only react less strongly to violence, but can also develop less accurate ideas about death and even show less fear of it (Slaughter and Griffiths, 2007, Mortality). While experts at Harvard Health note that overall youth crime rates haven't gone up with video game use, the concern is more about how games shape the way kids think and feel in everyday life (Harvard Health, 2010). For parents, this means paying close attention to the types of games children are playing and having open conversations about what they're seeing on screen, so kids don't lose sight of compassion and the real-world value of life.

Example: A 16-year-old girl confessed she no longer reacts when she sees disaster coverage online. "I just can't care about everything," she said flatly. Her parents worried this detachment was seeping into her real-life relationships.

6. The Loss of Patience

Patience used to be a learned skill, practiced daily. We waited for letters in the mail, for photos to be developed, for TV shows to air once a week. But in the digital age, nearly everything is instant—streaming, one-click shopping, on-demand food delivery. Amazon has conditioned us to expect next-day delivery; social media has conditioned us to expect likes within minutes.

The problem is that when children don't practice waiting, their tolerance for delay disappears. Patience is like a muscle: without use, it atrophies. Studies show that children accustomed to instant gratification are more prone to irritability, frustration, and difficulty sticking with long-term goals.

Example: A mom described how her son grew furious when a video game took 10 seconds to load. "It's broken!" he shouted, slamming the controller. Ten seconds felt unbearable to him—a reflection of how deeply impatience had taken root.

7. Superficial Relationships

On social media, it's easy to confuse connection with community. Teens may have hundreds, even thousands, of online "friends," but the majority of those connections are shallow. Real friendships require vulnerability, conflict resolution, and time. Social media interactions often bypass all three.

The language of friendship itself has shifted. The average Facebook user has around 338 "friends," yet loneliness among teens is at record highs. Online, ghosting has become a normal way to end a relationship. For adolescents who are just learning how to navigate intimacy, these digital shortcuts undermine the development of authentic, lasting bonds.

Example: A 15-year-old girl told her mom she had "tons of friends" online. But when asked whom she could call if she was upset at midnight, she admitted, "Probably no one."

8. Life as Performance

Smartphones have turned ordinary life into a stage. Instead of experiencing moments directly, children often document them for an audience, whether that audience is their peers or strangers online. The unconscious question becomes: "How will this look on Instagram?" instead of "How does this feel to me?"

The compulsion to document erodes mindfulness. Studies suggest the average person stores nearly 3,000 photos on their phone, most of which are rarely viewed. By curating rather than experiencing, children miss the richness of the present moment and risk tethering their self-worth to external validation.

Example: At his birthday party, a boy spent more time posing for photos than playing games with friends. Later, when his parents asked what his favorite part of the party was, he couldn't name one. He was too busy performing to actually enjoy it.

9. Shrinking Attention Spans

The rapid-fire pace of digital content reshapes the brain. Platforms like TikTok and YouTube train kids to crave novelty every few seconds. This makes focusing on a book, lecture, or conversation feel dull by comparison.

Researchers have noted that average attention spans are declining, with many children struggling to sustain focus beyond short bursts. In classrooms, teachers report rising difficulty keeping students engaged with complex material. Without the ability to concentrate deeply, children miss out on developing expertise, resilience, and intellectual curiosity.

Example: A teacher asked her students to read a chapter silently. Within minutes, several had pulled out their phones "just for a second." One later admitted, "I can't read a whole chapter anymore without needing a break."

10. The Vanishing Joy of Anticipation

Anticipation is a natural source of joy—waiting for a holiday, saving up for a big purchase, or looking forward to seeing a loved one. Delayed gratification strengthens resilience and makes the eventual reward more meaningful. But when nearly everything is available instantly, that pleasure is disappearing.

Today's children are rarely asked to wait. Movies, music, games, and shopping are all instantly available on demand. This erodes the ability to savor the build-up of anticipation and can diminish the overall capacity for joy.

Example: A boy used to count down the days to his birthday, buzzing with excitement. But when gifts could be ordered online and delivered the next day, he shrugged. The magic of waiting had been lost.

11. Losing the Art of Face-to-Face Communication

Conversation is an art form: reading body language, pausing, making eye contact, listening actively. Yet children raised on screens often spend far more time texting or gaming than speaking face-to-face.U.S. time-diary data show that today's teens devote much more of their day to on-screen leisure than to face-to-face conversation. In 2024, 15–19-year-olds averaged about 1.31 hours/day playing games or using a computer for leisure but only 0.59 hours/day socializing in person; time counted as "telephone, mail, and email"—which includes texting and internet voice/video calling—averaged 0.25 hours/day. Surveys also find that digital messaging is used daily far more often than in-person meetups with friends (55% of teens text friends every day vs. 25% who see friends in person daily outside school), underscoring a shift toward screen-mediated interaction. Peer-reviewed analyses of national time diaries further document substantial declines in non-digital (in-person) social interaction among adolescents since the mid-2000s, consistent with rising screen engagement.

Without practice, children lose the subtleties of in-person communication.

Research shows that nonverbal cues account for up to 70% of communication. Emojis and GIFs can't replace tone, posture, or facial expression. Teachers and employers increasingly report seeing young people struggle with basic social skills, from interviewing to engaging in small talk.

Example: A high schooler texted her mom from her bedroom to ask what was for dinner—while they were under the same roof. The shortcut was convenient, but over time this kind of digital substitution erodes the depth and warmth of human connection.

12. Gaming Addiction

Video games are designed to be immersive, rewarding, and quite addictive. With sophisticated reinforcement loops—level-ups, achievements, virtual rewards—games provide constant stimulation that can hijack the brain's dopamine system. For vulnerable children, this can spiral into full-blown addiction.

The World Health Organization has even recognized "gaming disorder" as a diagnosable condition. Studies estimate that 3% of gamers experience symptoms consistent with addiction, including neglecting school, relationships, and even physical health.

Example: A 14-year-old boy began skipping soccer practice to play his favorite online game. Eventually, he stopped leaving his room altogether. His parents only realized the depth of the problem when his grades plummeted, and he admitted he hadn't slept properly in weeks.

13. Online Bullying

Unlike traditional bullying, which often ends when a child leaves school for the day, online bullying follows kids into their bedrooms. Harassment can be constant, anonymous, and amplified by an audience. According to the National Institutes for Health, cyberbullying has been linked to increased rates of anxiety, depression, and suicidal thoughts among adolescents.

Suicide Rates for Younger Adolescents

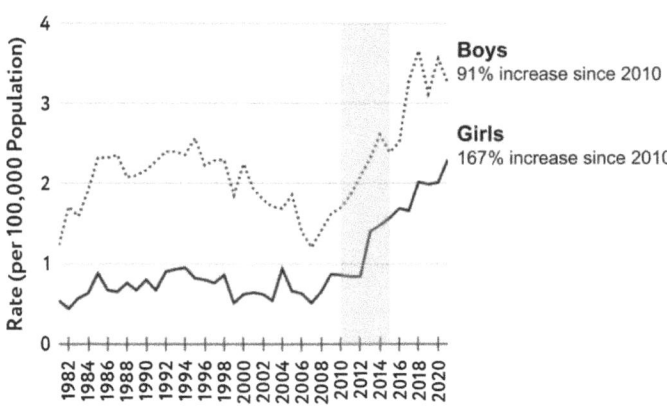

Figure 1.5. Suicide rates for U.S. adolescents, ages 10–14. (Source: U.S. Centers for Disease Control, National Center for Injury Prevention and Control.)[22]

According to the Pew Research Center, nearly 46% of teens say they've experienced cyberbullying in some form. For many, it's not just mean comments; it's the spreading of rumors or threats or the sharing of private photos.

Example: A middle schooler found that an unflattering photo of her had been turned into a cruel meme and shared widely. Even after her parents intervened, the damage was done: her self-esteem plummeted, and she dreaded returning to school.

14. Pornography Exposure

The Institute for Family Studies found that the average age of first exposure to online pornography is now 12 years old. For many kids, it happens accidentally while searching for something unrelated. Parents often underestimate how easily children stumble onto porn sites, even with basic filters in place. The accessibility of explicit content—often violent or unrealistic—can warp developing views of intimacy, relationships, and consent.

Science Direct clearly found that exposure at a young age has been linked to distorted expectations, difficulty forming healthy relationships, and even desensitization to violence.

Example: A parent was shocked when her 12-year-old son casually mentioned a graphic term he had picked up from a porn site. "I thought he was too young to even know what that meant," she admitted. In reality, he had been exposed months earlier through a link shared in a gaming chat.

15. The Decline of Creativity

Boredom used to be the breeding ground of creativity. With nothing to do, children invented games, wrote stories, or explored outside. Now, boredom is instantly filled with a screen. TikTok, YouTube, and video games offer endless stimulation, leaving little space for imagination.

Neuro Leadership Institute confirms that downtime is essential for the brain's "default mode network"—a system linked to creative thinking and problem-solving. Without unstructured time, children lose opportunities to daydream, experiment, and create.

Example: A father remembered how, as a child, he and his friends built elaborate forts out of cardboard boxes. His daughter, by contrast, spent her free time scrolling short videos. "She never has the chance to get bored enough to come up with something on her own," he said.

16. "Always On" Culture. Permanently connected to the Internet.

Teenagers growing up in an "always on" culture are pulled into a 24/7 stream of notifications, gossip, and comparison that keeps their brains revved when they should be resting and recovering. Many even sleep with a phone under the pillow, which fragments sleep, blunts memory and mood, and makes mornings feel like wading through wet cement. Constant pings splinter attention, training the mind to expect interruptions and making homework, conversation, and even hobbies feel boring by comparison. FOMO—fear of missing out—turns normal downtime into anxiety, as teens worry that if they're not online, they'll lose status, friendships, or opportunities. The highlight-reel effect on social media fuels relentless comparison, which can lower self-esteem and intensify loneliness even when a teen is technically "connected." Late-night scrolling pushes circadian rhythms later, raising irritability and stress while sapping motivation the next day. And with boundaries eroded, conflicts, rumors, and cyberbullying can reach a teen's pocket at any hour, leaving no safe space to reset. The same 24/7 connection also traps adults in perpetual "work mode"—answering texts and emails at midnight, on weekends, and even on vacation—until it becomes normalized and silently expected by employers and colleagues. When adults feel guilty or fear consequences for not replying instantly, that pressure trickles down to kids as the household's frenetic "always-on" default pace.

Example: A seventh grader plugs in her phone and tucks it under her pillow at 10 p.m., but a friend texts the group chat at 10:30; she grabs the phone "just for a minute," then spends an hour watching reels. By morning she feels wired and foggy, rushes through breakfast, and snaps at her mom, promising she'll "catch up" tomorrow—only to repeat the cycle that night.

17. Sleep Deprivation

Teens Who Get Less Than 7 Hours of Sleep

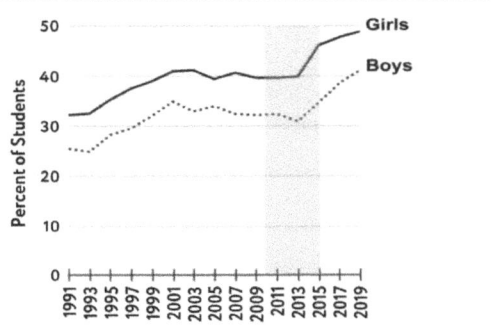

Figure 5.2. Percent of U.S. students (8th, 10th, and 12th grade) who get less than seven hours of sleep on most nights. (Source: Monitoring the Future.)[33]

As the data above, screens are stealing children's sleep. Between the blue light emitted by devices, the late-night urge to keep scrolling, and the anxiety stirred up by online interactions, many kids simply don't get enough sleep, sometimes as little as 3-4 hours per night. The American Academy of Pediatrics reports that 75% of teens aren't getting the recommended 8–10 hours of sleep per night.

Sleep deprivation isn't just about being tired. It disrupts mood regulation, weakens immunity, and impairs learning. One study found that high schoolers who got less than six hours of sleep per night were twice as likely to report depression symptoms compared to their well-rested peers.

Example: A mom discovered her daughter was hiding her phone under her pillow to check Snapchat after lights out. Night after night, she stayed up until 2 a.m., exhausted but unable to disconnect. "It's like she was addicted," her mom said.

18. Consumerism and Materialism

Social media platforms double as marketplaces, pushing ads, influencers, and trends at kids around the clock. Science Direct Research found that this constant barrage equates self-worth with what you buy, wear, or own. Studies show that heavy exposure to online advertising is linked to increased materialism and lower life satisfaction in adolescents.

Instead of valuing experiences, relationships, or achievements, children may learn to measure themselves by the latest sneakers or gadgets. And because trends change so quickly, the chase for the "next thing" never ends.

Example: A 12-year-old begged his parents for $200 designer shoes after seeing all his favorite YouTubers wearing them. When his parents refused, he felt left out at school and declared, "Everyone will think I'm poor."

19. Echo Chambers and Radicalization

Algorithms are designed to keep users engaged by serving up more of what they already consume. For young people, this can quickly become an echo chamber, where the only voices they hear reinforce their existing beliefs or fears. In some cases, this environment fosters extremism or radicalization.

Researchers have documented how YouTube's recommendation engine can funnel users from harmless content into darker, more extreme material in just a few clicks. Teens, with their developing critical thinking skills, are especially vulnerable.

Example: A parent noticed that her son was becoming obsessed with conspiracy theories he found online. What began as harmless UFO videos spiraled into paranoia about government plots, isolating him from friends who didn't share his new worldview.

20. The Erosion of Family Time
Often Feel Lonely

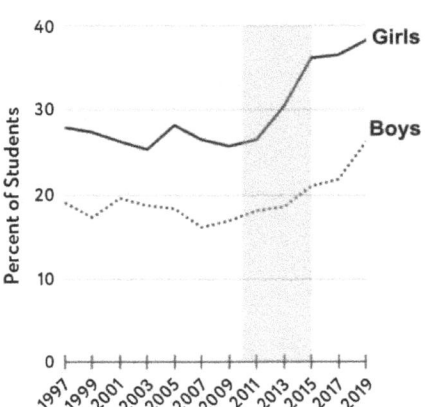

Figure 6.7. Percent of U.S. students (8th, 10th, and 12th grade) who agreed or mostly agreed with the statement "A lot of times I feel lonely." (Source: Monitoring the Future.)

Perhaps the most heartbreaking danger is the slow erosion of family connection. Dinner tables once hosted conversations: now they're filled with the glow of individual screens. Family trips, movie nights, or even car rides risk being fragmented by constant digital interruptions.

Children learn about trust, belonging, and values through time with their families. When that time is replaced with scrolling or gaming, opportunities to build resilience and emotional security slip away. The result isn't just disconnection - it's loneliness. Even while you're all sitting in the same room.

Example: One mom described family dinners as "everyone eating together, but alone." Her son watched YouTube, her daughter texted friends, and her husband scrolled emails. "We were all there physically," she said, "but not really together."

AI: An Existential Threat

While the subject of the rapid emergence of AI and its influence on our young people deserves its own book, we still must mention the most current information available to the authors at the time of publication.

While AI promises gains in productivity and dramatically cuts delivery times (i.e., shortcuts), it hollows critical linear thinking and research skills for frequent users. When tools draft ideas for our students, they skip the mental "reps" that build memory, judgment, and grit—like a muscle, the brain atrophies when it isn't used. That worry isn't abstract: Pew reports that 26% of U.S. teens used ChatGPT for schoolwork in 2024–2025, doubling from 2023—evidence that offloading cognition is becoming routine (Pew Research Center, 2024).

Academic integrity is a big problem now. In 2023–2024, 63% of teachers said students got in trouble for being accused of using generative AI on schoolwork, and preventing AI-enabled cheating has become a top faculty challenge, according to Turnitin. These patterns normalize "getting answers" over learning how to think, study, and recall core facts habits students need for exams, careers, and critical life skills (Education Week, 2023; Bizzabo, 2024).

Layered on top is screen and digital addiction. Since the early 2010s smartphone shift, adolescent anxiety, and depression have climbed sharply. The CDC's Youth Risk Behavior data show sustained increases in persistent sadness and related risks, while the U.S. Surgeon General warns that social media exposure can harm youths' mental health. Jonathan Haidt's book, The Anxious Generation, crystallizes this timeline and argues that the "phone-based childhood" has displaced sleep, play, and in-person connection—conditions for healthy minds (CDC, 2023; HHS.gov, 2023; Haidt, 2024). The takeaway we can offer here is to use AI very sparingly, for students to do their own thinking and writing, and for parents to set firm boundaries on screens so learning (and well-being) can develop in a healthy way.

Beyond Plagiarism: AI's Broader Risks

Most people think the big problem with AI is plagiarism. Ironically, that may be the least consequential issue. A far greater concern is that AI is eroding our ability to tell what is real and what is fake. Generative AI now produces "deepfakes"—false but highly realistic videos, images, and audio—that are almost impossible to distinguish from reality. These tools can be used to impersonate people, spread disinformation, or manipulate democratic processes, and even AI itself acknowledges this risk (Chesney and Citron, 2019). The danger is not simply cheating on a test but undermining the very foundations of trust in what we see and hear.

The greatest threats posed by AI range from immediate concerns like job displacement and the spread of misinformation to long-term existential risks to humanity itself. Many of these problems stem from the biases in the data used to train AI systems and the complexity of their decision-making processes, which even experts may not fully understand (Bender et al., 2021). As a result, we face not just individual harms, but broad societal challenges that include ethics, governance, and the future stability of human institutions.

Societal and Ethical Threats
- AI often reproduces human biases, which can reinforce discrimination in areas like hiring, policing, and lending unless closely monitored.
- Deepfakes and AI-generated misinformation are powerful tools for manipulation, threatening democracy and eroding public trust.
- The vast data demands of AI raise serious privacy concerns, leaving individuals vulnerable to exploitation and state surveillance.
- Automation powered by AI is displacing many traditional jobs, potentially worsening inequality without major efforts in retraining.
- Because AI systems often operate as "black boxes," accountability becomes unclear when they make harmful or life-altering decisions.

Security and Control Threats
- AI is transforming cybersecurity by enabling faster, more adaptive, and harder-to-detect cyberattacks that endanger digital infrastructure.
- Autonomous weapons lower the barriers to armed conflict, creating new risks for global instability and warfare.
- The prospect of superintelligent AI poses an existential threat if its goals diverge from human values and control is lost.

Environmental and Economic Threats
- The enormous energy and water use of AI makes it a significant and growing environmental burden.
- In global finance, AI-driven trading can destabilize mar-

kets, creating the risk of sudden crashes and large-scale economic crises.

Final Note: AI is Moving Too Fast

AI is not just a schoolyard issue — it is reshaping economies, societies, and even human identity. The technology is evolving so rapidly that what we write today could be outdated tomorrow. That in itself is a danger: institutions, parents, and educators may not be able to adapt quickly enough to protect young people or society at large (Cave and Dignum, 2019).

What can we do? We can try to become aware of all the ways that people may be using AI unknowingly, think critically, use it as little as we can, and try our best to not outsource our humanity to machines.

In Summary

Digital technology has undeniable benefits. But the hidden costs—ranging from eroded patience and empathy to exposure to pornography and manipulation by algorithms—are profound.

This is not about blaming parents or shaming kids. Digital addiction is not a character flaw. Like all addictions, it preys on brain chemistry—and Big Tech has engineered it to be irresistible.

The good news: change is possible. Families can reclaim balance. Children can rediscover patience, curiosity, and connection. Parents, armed with insight, can help their kids thrive in an increasingly digital world.

In the next chapter, we'll explore how understanding your child's personality type gives you a powerful tool to protect them—and to rebuild the strong, trusting bond that is the best defense against digital addiction.

CHAPTER 3
Personality Type: Why we are who we are

Wow! Your head must be spinning, having just learned how anxiety and depression among children and adolescents has skyrocketed, the devastating impact it's having on children and families, and how this problem has been made so much worse by digital addiction.

You'll find this chapter much more hopeful, as we introduce a fascinating new way of understanding your child and show you how to create the kind of supportive relationship your child needs to protect their mental health by creating the most trusting, healthy relationship possible.

Mental health professionals have struggled for decades to better understand the causes of childhood anxiety and depression and to find effective strategies to prevent and treat them. The conventional wisdom is that the major risk factors are trauma and stressful life events, alcohol and drug use, loss of an important relationship, environmental factors (including family problems), family history (including other family members who suffer from depression), neurodevelopmental disorders (ADHD, autism, learning disabilities, and others), and physical illness or a serious medical condition.

These are all established risk factors. However, psychological researchers have failed to study what may be the single most consequential risk factor of all: an individual's innate personality type.

What do you mean by "personality type"?

First, what we're not talking about is the over-simplified theory that divides people into two categories, Type A or Type B, developed by cardiologists to determine if a person may be more vulnerable to heart problems.

What we are describing is a well-researched, widely respected, comprehensive system for understanding people called the Jung/Myers Model of personality type. Devised by Swiss psychologist Carl Jung, it was greatly expanded upon and popularized by the American mother-and-daughter team of Katherine Briggs and Isabel Briggs Myers, who created the Myers-Briggs Type Indicator. The "MBTI" is the most widely used personality type assessment in the world, estimated to have been taken by more than fifty million people.

In the Jung/Myers model, there are four components, or "dimensions," that make up an individual's personality type: how people are energized (being with others or by reflecting alone), what kind of information they naturally notice and remember (concrete and specific or more abstract and imaginative), how they make decisions, (logically and impersonally or more influenced by their own and others' feelings), and how they like to organize the world around them (more organized and decisive or more open-ended and spontaneous).

Please note: Many people think of "personality type" and the MBTI as interchangeable terms. But the MBTI (or Myers-Briggs) refers to the assessment that identifies a person's type, while the personality type model is a rich, comprehensive theory.

Are people born with a type, and does it change over time?

Having studied, researched, and written extensively about the Jung/Myers model for more than forty-five years, Paul Tieger – co-author of this book – strongly believes people are born with one specific personality type that never changes. This is not to say that people don't change as they remains constant throughout life, and experience new things. Hopefully, we act differently at a basketball game than at a funeral. But that doesn't mean our personality type has changed—only certain behaviors. And human beings have a wide range of behaviors available to them, many of which are influenced by their innate personality type.

What evidence supports this assertion? Surprisingly, there has been no scientific research examining whether type is inborn or based on experience. But, if you have children or siblings, ask yourself, "Are their personalities more similar to or different from each other's? Or is the adult version of you fundamentally more similar to or different from the younger version?" Most people would say "more similar." In other words, our central qualities (our type) remain the same throughout our lives. As one example, barring unusual trauma, children who are lighthearted and funny tend also to be that way when they grow up. Just as serious, cautious children most often retain that demeanor as adults.

Personality is a combination of nature—our inborn personality type—and nurture —everything else, including our gender, race, ethnicity, socio-economic status, education, and, most importantly, our parents and how we were parented.

While type theory is not settled science, one does not have to agree that type is inborn to find the insights it provides enormously valuable, since the vast majority of psychologists and early childhood educators believe that by the time a child is seven, "the cake is baked" and their personalities are formed in the most significant ways.

If you've taken the MBTI at different times in your life and have gotten different results, you may think that your type has changed. But there are several good reasons that this may happen. You might have taken the assessment at work, rather than at home (a truer indication of who you are), you might have been going through a particularly stressful time, or you might have answered the assessment questions the way you thought you were supposed to, perhaps for employment purposes. The point is, just because you came out with different test results, that doesn't mean your type has changed.

What are the five personality types described in this book?

In the Jung/Myers Model, there are sixteen personality types. But in ReConnect, there are only five. Here's why.

The focus of this book is on how personality type may predispose some people to anxiety and depression, based on robust research described below. One key finding was that not all of the four Jung/Myers personality type dimensions play a role in such predisposition. Statistical analysis revealed that only five types included the relevant characteristics that do play such a role.

Here is a snapshot of the five types. In just a few moments, you will learn much more about each by taking the assessment that will help you identify your and your child's personality types.

Type 1: Responsible Hard Workers

Make up about 46% of the U.S. population. Their core value include working hard, doing the right thing, and being of service. They tend to be serious, dependable, and organized, follow rules, like routines, seek closure, and respect authority figures.

Type 2: Strategic Problem Solvers

Make up only about 10% of the U.S. population. Their core values include learning, being competent, and achieving success. They tend to love learning and to be intellectually curious, success-driven, confident, logical, objective, and prone to "push back."

Type 3: Adventurous Free Spirits

Make up about 18% of the U.S. population. Their core values include enjoying their lives, being present, and being free to act spontaneously. They tend to be playful, spontaneous, physical / athletic, impulsive, risk-taking, competitive, and non-conformist.

Type 4: Gentle Humble Helpers

Make up only about 9% of the U.S. population. Their core values include living in the moment, tuning into others' needs, and being helpful in real and practical ways. They tend to be sensitive, warm, nurturing, playful, accommodating, easy-going, and conflict avoidant.

Type 5: Creative Sensitive Souls

Make up about 17% of the U.S. population. Their core values include being authentic, finding meaning, and helping people develop their potential. They tend to be empathetic, perceptive, idealistic, compassionate, "artsy" / alternative, harmony-seeking, and prone to worry.

How is knowing about personality type helpful?

While personality type does not explain everything, it does explain a lot about human behavior: important things like what motivates us, what we value, how we prefer to be communicated with, how we parent, which careers we find most satisfying, our politics, who we're attracted to, and why some relationships work and others don't. But most relevant to this book is which personality types may be at greatest risk for anxiety and depression and how parents of all children can build the healthiest, most satisfying relationships possible.

Is there a danger of stereotyping a person based on their personality type? Unfortunately, stereotyping based on gender, race, age, ethnic background, sexual orientation, socio-economic status, or geography occurs all too frequently. So, the short answer is, yes, there is a risk. However, an important underlying principle of personality type is that while people of the same type may be similar in many ways, every individual is unique! By keeping this fact front of mind, we can avoid the temptation to pre-judge a person based on their personality type.

Is there scientific evidence linking personality type with anxiety and depression?

The answer is yes, and the evidence is compelling! Paul Tieger collaborated on a first-of-its-kind study with the University of Minnesota College of Pharmacy. The data showed that two of the five types were significantly more likely to suffer from severe anxiety and depression than the other three types. These two types make up about 25% of the U.S. population and include about 6.5 million children between the ages of 10 and 17.

Percentage of US Population by Personality type

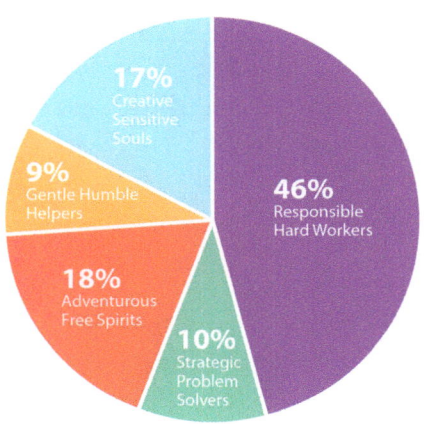

This graphic illustrates the degree to which the five types report severe anxiety and depression in a large, representation sample involving 10,500 people.

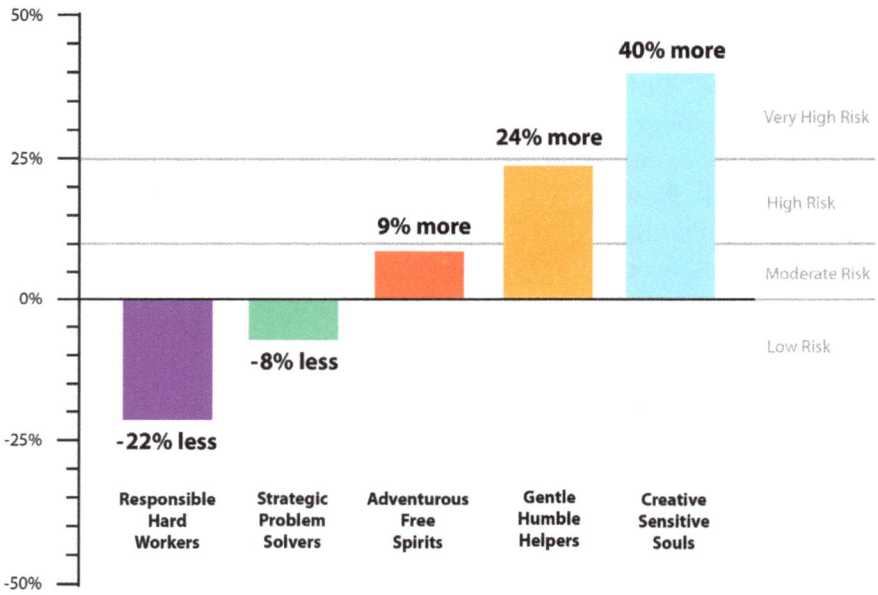

Proportion of personality types reporting more or less Severe Anxiety and Depression (A & D) than expected *

**Depression using the PHQ-4 by Personality Type (n = 10,500)

Copyright @2024 Paul D. Tieger. All rights reserved.

Does this mean that if your child is a Gentle Humble Helper or Creative Sensitive Soul, they are at increased risk? Not necessarily. Nor does it mean that if they are one of the other three types, they are at decreased risk. Type is not destiny! The key point is that in either case, parents are often astonished at how much better they understand their child once they discover their personality type.

Who is this book for?

We believe that ReConnect can be extremely helpful for children, families, and the people who support them, including grandparents, pediatricians, school counselors, psychologists, and other care givers.

Please note that while the personality type assessment in this book has been validated to be more than 90% accurate, it has not been validated for children with neurodevelopmental disorders such as Autism Spectrum Disorder (ASD) and Attention-Deficit/Hyperactivity Disorder (ADHD), learning disabilities, intellectual disabilities, and communication disorders. Therefore, if your child has been diagnosed with any of these conditions, the personality type results may not accurately identify their personality type. However, the assessment should accurately identify your personality type and provide you with fresh new insights into you, insights that can affect the way you understand and relate to your child.

CHAPTER 4
Who am I? Who are you? Who are we?
Identifying your and your child's personality types

Now the fun begins!

Below are brief descriptions of the five personality types. In most cases your type and your child's will be different, although they may be the same.

Each description begins with five bullet points that list that type's central characteristics. It then notes how those characteristics look in children, and then in adults.

To use this information, please:

- Review the five bullets for ALL five types. If one type sounds more like you, or your child, continue to read about how this type looks "In Children" and "In Adults."
- If about 80% of one type's description sounds like you or your child, you have probably identified your and their most likely types. (NO profile will sound 100% like either of you!)
- To confirm that you've identified your most likely types, we suggest you take a few minutes to review the remaining types.
- When you've identified your and your child's most likely types, make a note of that combination. For example, you may be a Responsible Hard Worker, and your child may be a Gentle Humble Helper—or any one of the 24 other combinations.
- Turn to page 58 to find your way to your customized Parent-Child Personality Type Profile.

If, after reviewing your Parent-Child Personality Type Profile, either your or your child's type does not seem to fit, you might want to go back to this chapter and take a second look at the five types and see if one feels like a better fit for you or your child.

Type 1: Responsible Hard Workers
Make up about 46% of the U.S. population

Children and parents who are Responsible Hard Workers share many of the same qualities, key motivations, and core values. They tend to:

- Be serious and cautious
- Follow the rules and want others to do so, too
- Respect authority figures like parents, teachers, doctors, and police officers
- Like to plan ahead and get upset if plans are changed – especially at the last minute
- Finish whatever they start, whether it's a work project, a game or puzzle, or a book

In Children:

Responsible Hard Worker children tend to be realistic and down to earth, preferring to talk about real things rather than abstract ideas. They find consistent routines comforting and usually enjoy participating in holidays and other traditions. Reliable, dependable, and conscientious, they typically enjoy caring for siblings and pets. These children tend to be cooperative when it comes to doing chores or finishing their homework, and they enjoy routines and familiar ways of doing things.

Responsible Hard Worker children are generally cautious and don't usually jump into new experiences quickly. They also like being productive and often feel compelled to finish what they start, whether it's a game or chore. Some Responsible Hard Worker children are more sensitive than others, and these children seldom push back or challenge authority figures. Others are more logical and can be quite assertive. But the core characteristics described above are the same for both versions.

In Adults:

Responsible Hard Worker parents tend to be traditional and conventional. They often like being of service and are likely to volunteer for service clubs, religious organizations, hospitals, charity drives, and other causes. They tend to be straightforward and down to earth: what you see is what you get, and their word is their bond.

Responsible Hard Workers are usually good at noticing when something needs fixing, coming up with a practical solution, and applying their experience to get the job done. They tend to resist change, with many preferring, if possible, to stay in the same job or home for a long time. They are most comfortable working in a structured environment with clear instructions and expectations, where they are rewarded for working hard and meeting their employer's goals. Some common occupations include management, sales, law, business, law enforcement, trades, education, operations, finance, healthcare, engineering, and computer science.

Type 2: Strategic Problem Solvers

Make up about 10% of the U.S. population

Children and parents who are Strategic Problem Solvers share many of the same qualities, key motivations, and core values. They tend to:

- Be independent, strategic, and competitive

- Be life-long learners who are creative and who place a high value on competence

- Like to debate issues and push back to clarify a question or make a point

- Be confident and have strong opinions

- Be logical, objective, and not especially emotional or overly affectionate

In Children:

Strategic Problem Solver children tend to be independent and curious and are usually good at whatever activities interest them. Because they love learning and tend to be quick studies, they are usually good students, but they can get bored when they're not challenged enough. Strategic Problem Solver children can be tricky to parent because they learn by questioning things and often like to argue or push back, especially when something doesn't make sense or seem fair to them. They usually come across as confident and self-assured, but they may also appear somewhat aloof, and they often don't show affection easily. Some Strategic Problem Solver children may be more organized and decisive, while others may be more spontaneous and playful. But the core characteristics described above are the same for both versions.

In Adults:

Strategic Problem Solver parents tend to be high achievers. Because they love learning, have quick minds, grasp complex ideas quickly, and are energized by challenges, they often end up in leadership positions. They connect the dots quite easily and can usually see how most things can be improved. Driven to excel at whatever they do, they set high standards for themselves—and often for their children. Confident and self-assured, Strategic Problem Solver parents often gravitate to work that allows them to be independent, continue to learn and be intellectually challenged, solve problems creatively, and advance in the organization while being recognized and well-compensated for their competence. Specific fields that often attract this type include college-level teaching, research, law, technology, economics and finance, science, psychiatry, architecture, and consulting.

Type 3: Adventurous Free Spirits

Make up about 18% of the U.S. population

Children and parents who are Adventurous Free Spirits share many of the same qualities, key motivations, and core values. They tend to:

- Love to have fun, enjoy their life, and not take things too seriously
- Like to be spontaneous, be impulsive, and take risks
- Like to win— and usually don't worry much about those who lose

- Enjoy sports, physical activities, and being in nature
- Not mind bending the rules

In Children:

Adventurous Free Spirit children tend to be playful and easy going. They enjoy living in the moment rather than planning too far in advance; nor do they worry much about the future. They love being free to spontaneously respond to whatever fun new activity presents itself. These kids tend to be more realistic than imaginative and usually like playing games they know—often those that involve objects such as bats, balls, dolls, water balloons, and the like. They may like to tease or play practical jokes on others without necessarily being aware as to whether the other enjoys the experience.

Adventurous Free Spirit children are often quite physical and would rather do something than discuss doing something. They can also be impulsive and take more risks than their parents are comfortable with. They learn best by doing rather than by reading or listening to people talking. The more physical and tactile the experience, the more lasting impression it will leave on them. Some Adventurous Free Spirit children may be more outgoing and friendly, while others may be more private and reserved. But the core characteristics described above are the same for both versions.

In Adults:

Most Adventurous Free Spirit parents enjoy living in the moment and love being free to spontaneously respond to new and fun opportunities. They are usually quite physical and often enjoy playing or watching sports or being in nature. Flexible and adaptable, they prefer not to plan too far in advance and can usually shift gears quickly. Observant about what's going on around them, many are skillful with tools and understand the mechanics of how things work. Practical and down to earth, Adventurous Free Spirit parents cherish their freedom, don't like being micromanaged, and are often very good in a crisis. And they usually don't have difficulty bending the rules when they think the situation calls for it.

One finds Adventurous Free Spirit parents in all occupations, but their work is more satisfying to them when it is fun and exciting, involves physical activity, gives them a lot of freedom, and doesn't require excessive supervision. Specific occupations that often attract these folks include first responder (police officer, firefighter, EMT), athletic coach, sports commentator, builder, trial attorney, tradesperson, surgeon, and stock trader.

Type 4: Gentle Humble Helpers
Make up about 9% of the U.S. population

Children and parents who are Gentle Humble Helpers share many of the same qualities, key motivations, and core values. They tend to:
- Be casual, easy going, warm, gentle, and kind
- Be playful, spontaneous, and impulsive
- Have deep feelings, but be private about them
- Like to please people, avoid conflict, and be loyal friends
- Be nurturing and take good care of children, pets, and those in need

In Children:

Gentle Humble Helper kids tend to be laid back, casual, and nurturing. They are very sensitive and feel things deeply but are likely to share their feelings only with people they trust. They love harmonious relationships and get nervous and anxious when there is conflict or when people are upset or angry with them. They are usually very good at sharing their toys and possessions with friends, seldom get into arguments or fights, and are usually very protective and nurturing of their siblings, younger children, or animals. Gentle Humble Helper children are playful and usually have a good sense of humor, and if they make a joke, it is seldom at someone else's expense. They like being spontaneous, responding to whatever fun thing comes up, and they feel uncomfortable making plans—especially far into the future. These are not terribly introspective kids, and they can be quite impulsive. It's not uncommon for them to do something that seems like a good idea… at the time. Some Gentle Humble Helper children may be more outgoing and friendly, while others may be more private and reserved. But the core characteristics described above are the same for both versions.

In Adults

Gentle Humble Helper parents are the ultimate care givers. Whether they're interacting with other adults, children, or animals, they are acutely attuned to how others are feeling and motivated to try to make them feel better or ease their discomfort. Realistic and practical, they tend to avoid conflict at all costs, and in their desire to please others, they can sometimes put others' needs ahead of their own. Gentle Humble Helper parents like best to live in the moment rather than make long-term plans.

One finds Gentle Humble Helper parents in all occupations, but they often gravitate to work that affords them a lot of freedom, variety, and flexibility and a casual, tension-free environment in which they get to help people or animals in real and practical ways. Specific occupations that attract people of this type include healthcare, EMT work, veterinary medicine, massage, physical and occupational therapy, and caring for children, the elderly or disabled, and animals.

Type 5: Creative Sensitive Souls

Make up about 17% of the U.S. population

Children and parents who are Creative Sensitive Souls share many of the same qualities, key motivations, and core values. They tend to:

- Be very sensitive and compassionate, to seek harmony and be idealistic
- Be empathetic, perceptive, loving, and affectionate
- Be creative and express themselves through writing, art, music, poetry, dance, acting, and other artistic pursuits
- Take things personally and become upset when criticized
- Be easily frightened and prone to worrying

In Children:

Because Creative Sensitive Souls feel things deeply and are so empathetic, they avoid conflict and try to make people happy, often putting others' needs ahead of their own. The combination of Creative Sensitive Soul children's vivid imaginations and their deep feelings make them the most idealistic of all types. They know the way things should be, but seldom are, which can cause them to become disappointed, moody, disillusioned, or depressed. Often described as "artsy," these kids are often drawn to unique or alternative ways of thinking, acting, or dressing. Many are also easily frightened and prone to worrying. And because these children are so sensitive and see the world differently than many others, they can feel lonely and sometimes believe that they don't quite belong.

Many Creative Sensitive Souls have rich imaginations, and when they're young they may initiate play with "Let's pretend...." They usually take things personally and are easily upset when criticized. Typically, they are loving and physically affectionate but can be easily frightened and prone to worrying. Some Creative Sensitive Soul children may be more outgoing and friendly, while others may be more private and reserved. But the core characteristics described above are the same for both versions.

In Adults:

Creative Sensitive Soul parents are natural counselors. It's not unusual for friends, family members, colleagues, or even neighborhood children to seek them out because they are so understanding, empathetic, and caring and have such good communication skills. Most of these parents are open to new ideas and ways of looking at the world and encourage their children to think outside the box and try new things. Being extremely empathetic, they are also prone to anxiety and depression and tend to be worriers. They typically avoid conflict and, to make people happy, can put others' needs ahead of their own. They can also take things personally and become moody and easily upset when criticized.

One finds Creative Sensitive Souls in all occupations, but they often gravitate to work that involves understanding and helping people grow and develop their potential, makes use of their often-considerable creativity, and is in service of a mission in which they believe strongly. Specific fields that attract many people of this type include psychology, counseling, teaching of the humanities, writing, acting, journalism, producing, marketing, advertising, and human resources.

Find the chapter which describes you and your child.

	Adult Type 1: Responsible Hard Worker	Adult Type 2: Strategic Problem Solver	Adult Type 3: Adventurous Free Spirit	Adult Type 4: Gentle Humble Helpers	Adult Type 5: Creative Sensistive Souls
Child Type 1: Responsible Hard Worker	Chapter 5 pages 60 - 64	Chapter 10 pages 90 - 95	Chapter 15 pages 121 - 127	Chapter 20 pages 154 - 159	Chapter 25 pages 185 - 190
Child Type 2: Strategic Problem Solver	Chapter 6 pages 65 - 70	Chapter 11 pages 96 - 101	Chapter 16 pages 128 - 133	Chapter 21 pages 160 - 165	Chapter 26 pages 191 - 196
Child Type 3: Adventurous Free Spirit	Chapter 7 pages 71 - 76	Chapter 12 pages 102 - 107	Chapter 17 pages 134 - 139	Chapter 22 pages 166 - 171	Chapter 27 pages 197 - 202
Child Type 4: Gentle Humble Helpers	Chapter 8 pages 77 - 82	Chapter 13 pages 108 - 113	Chapter 18 pages 140 - 145	Chapter 23 pages 172 - 177	Chapter 28 pages 203 - 209
Child Type 5: Creative Sensistive Souls	Chapter 9 pages 83 - 88	Chapter 14 pages 114 - 119	Chapter 19 pages 146 - 152	Chapter 24 pages 178 - 183	Chapter 29 pages 210 - 215

Responsible Hard Worker Parent

and their Child Personality Types

CHAPTER 5
Responsible Hard Worker Parent & Child (Type1)

Of course, you know your child better than anyone! But with some types of children, regardless of how diligent the parent is, it's almost impossible to know what's going on beneath the surface. This Parent/Child Profile provides important new insights into your child, yourself, and how your similarities and differences affect your interactions, all with an eye toward helping you build the healthiest, most fulfilling relationship possible.

It's relatively rare for children and parents to share the same personality type, but when they do, the two are usually similar in many ways. Personality is a combination of nature—your inborn personality type—and nurture—everything else you experience in life, the greatest influence being your parents. While you and your child may be kindred spirits in many ways, there will be profound differences between the two of you because every person is a unique individual and because of your different ages, generations, experiences, and, most importantly, who you were parented by.

Here is a snapshot of the personality type you share with your child. If after reading this report you think that you may have misidentified your own or your child's type, you may want to revisit Chapter 4.

Your and your child's personality type:

Responsible Hard Worker
Always trying to do the right thing.

Responsible Hard Workers tend to be serious and cautious. By their nature, they tend to be comfortable with structure, boundaries, and following the rules, and they expect others to follow them, too.

Responsible Hard Workers usually respect authority figures such as parents, teachers, doctors, and police officers, and they tend not to push the envelope or rock the boat. As team players, they have a strong sense of duty and often feel an obligation to help others and to be of service, often participating in service clubs and volunteering for not-for-profit organizations or religious houses of worship. They are planners who can become annoyed when plans are changed, especially at the last minute. Their word is their bond. They have a strong work ethic and pride themselves on finishing whatever they start. They often make to-do lists and like to check off completed tasks.

As children and adolescents, Responsible Hard Workers are usually not especially challenging to parent. They tend to be fairly compliant when it comes to doing their chores, finishing their homework, and helping out with younger siblings. They usually take their responsibilities, such as caring for their pets, seriously.

One finds Responsible Hard Workers in all occupations, but they often gravitate to work that is fairly structured, provides clear instructions and expectations, and encourages and rewards them for working hard and meeting their employer's goals. Specific fields that attract people of this type include management, the law, business, law enforcement, education, operations, finance, healthcare, engineering, and computer science.

Responsible Hard Workers represent about 46% of the general population, making them the most common personality type.

Similarities with your child

In general, the more similar two people's personality types, the easier the relationship. Not necessarily better, but easier. The three components of personality in which people can be most similar or different are the way they perceive the world, their core motivators, and their preferred communication style.

An important commonality for parents and children who are both Responsible Hard Workers is that you both take in information in a similar way, primarily relying on your five senses, which tends to make you realistic, practical, detail-oriented, and down-to-earth people.

When two people of the same type do experience conflict, it's often because they are too similar, having similar weaknesses and blind spots. Weaknesses are those things we know we're not good at, while blind spots are things we are unaware of that cause us to not be as effective as we'd like to be.

For all people, it's not unusual to notice a quality or behavior in someone else that annoys us. Ironically, this is often because we share that same quality but may not be aware of, or able to own, it. This can be especially true when two people share the same personality type. It can feel like we're looking in the mirror—and don't always like what we see.

Most Responsible Hard Workers have strong opinions, based on an equally strong value system, which tends to make them see things in black and white rather than in shades of gray. This can lead them to believe there is only one best way to do things: their way. So, when there's a difference of opinion, both parents and children of this type tend to dig in and can be quite stubborn, and both may have a hard time backing down, even when doing so might end up producing the best result. But if you have more than one child, each with a different personality type (which is most often the case), you probably already know that to some extent all children need to be parented somewhat differently. This can cause consternation for your Responsible Hard Worker child, who seeks consistency and can be obsessed with the importance of fairness.

Responsible Hard Workers (both children and adults) come in two varieties. Some, those we call Feelers, are naturally more sensitive and nurturing, while others, the Thinkers, are more logical and analytical. If you and your child are both Thinkers or both Feelers, the relationship is usually easier. But if the parent is a Thinker and the child is Feeler, that parent needs to pay special attention to how the child is feeling in order to make the strongest connection. If both parent and child are Thinkers, this is generally an easier relationship to navigate. What if the parent is a Feeler and the child is a Thinker? The parent may not receive as much affection as they would like, and the child may push back more than the parent is comfortable with.

How this may play out in your relationship

All parents want what's best for their children. And often, mostly unconsciously, parents believe their children will be happier and more successful by being more like them.

Many child psychologists believe that the happiest, healthiest children are those whose parents really understand and appreciate them for the unique individuals they are. This fosters the child's self-esteem. Of course, the opposite is also true: when children are not seen for who they are or appreciated and celebrated for their gifts, they often grow up not feeling good about themselves—or not good enough, in general. It's important for parents who share the same type with their child to remember that while they may think like you, they may sound like you, they may even look like you, they are not you. It's easy for some parents to think of their child as a "mini-me," which can cause conflict.

While sharing the same personality type with your child is usually a big advantage, it can also present challenges, if for example you expect them to be as responsible, organized, diligent, on time, or tidy as you. It's important to remember that it took you decades to become that way!

How to nurture your child

"Meet your child where they are." Great advice: easy to give, but much harder to do! Stretching outside of your comfort zone is hard and may take some practice, especially when the stretching required means thinking about and employing skills that don't come naturally to the parent. But it is no less important than making sure your child is safe, clothed, or fed, and it may be more critical to protecting their mental health and promoting their wellbeing.

We all have gifts that make us special, characteristics for which we want and need to be appreciated. As a Responsible Hard Worker, among the things you probably value most about yourself is your sense of responsibility, duty, dedication to doing the right thing, and being of service to others. Your Responsible Hard Worker child has many of those same qualities, so it shouldn't be especially difficult to reinforce and appreciate those shared values and behaviors.

As we touched on earlier, if your Responsible Hard Worker child is more of a Feeler, they will respond best if you tune in to how they're feeling before trying to fix the problem, which is the natural instinct for most Responsible Hard Workers. But if both parent and child are Feelers, there is a danger that neither will be as honest about their feelings as would be helpful, for fear of upsetting the other.

When trying to engage your Responsible Hard Worker child in a conversation, they are more likely to respond to specific questions rooted in reality rather than hypothetical ones that require them to use their imagination. For example, if you ask them "What do you think Jason will do if you tell him he hurt your feelings?" you're likely to be met with a blank stare, followed by "I don't know." (Because they don't.) But if you ask them "Have you told Jason that he hurt your feelings?" followed by "What did he say (or do)?," you'll have a better chance of getting them to provide additional information that will help you have a more productive conversation.

With that said, here are:

Tried and true suggestions for engaging your
Responsible Hard Worker:

- Be clear and explicit in your directions and requests; say what you mean and mean what you say.
- Prepare them in advance for new experiences and changes in plans.
- Recognize you both want to be, and often are, right. Learn to back off and to choose your battles.
- Be on time; follow through on all your commitments to them.
- Encourage them to question things rather than always taking things at face value.
- Reward them with increasing levels of responsibility and praise them for their accomplishments.

This information is provided for educational purposes only and is not meant to diagnose any condition, or explain or predict any future behavior or conditions in children or adults of any personality type, as each person is a unique individual.

CHAPTER 6
Responsible Hard Worker Parent (Type 1) & Strategic Problem Solver Child (Type 2)

Of course, you know your child better than anyone! But with some types of children, regardless of how diligent the parent is, it's almost impossible to know what's going on beneath the surface. This Parent/Child Profile provides important new insights into your child, yourself, and how your similarities and differences affect your interactions, all with an eye toward helping you build the healthiest, most fulfilling relationship possible.

Your personality type:

Responsible Hard Worker
Always trying to do the right thing.

Responsible Hard Workers tend to be serious and cautious. They like familiar routines and traditions. By their nature, they like structure, boundaries, and following the rules, and they expect others to follow them, too.

Responsible Hard Workers usually respect authority figures such as parents, teachers, doctors, and police officers and tend not to push the envelope or rock the boat. As team players, they have a strong sense of duty and often feel an obligation to help others and to be of service. They often volunteer for service clubs or religious houses of worship. They are planners who can become annoyed when plans are changed, especially at the last minute. Their word is their bond. They have a strong work ethic and pride themselves on finishing whatever they start. They often make to-do lists and like to check off completed tasks.

One finds Responsible Hard Workers in all occupations, but

they often gravitate to work that is fairly structured, provides clear instructions and expectations, and encourages and rewards them for working hard and meeting their employer's goals. Specific fields that attract many people of this type include management, the law, business, law enforcement, teaching, operations, finance, healthcare, engineering, and computer science.

Responsible Hard Workers represent about 46% of the population, making them the most common personality type.

Your child's personality type:

Strategic Problem Solver
Everything can be improved.

Strategic Problem Solvers tend to be independent, strong-willed, and competitive. Their thirst for knowledge and love of learning drives them to excel and often results in their being high achievers. Their thought process can be complex, and they connect most dots quite easily. As a result, they love to figure things out and find ways to improve upon them, and they are usually gifted at doing so.

Strategic Problem Solvers can be challenging to parent because they often like to argue or push back, especially when something doesn't make sense or seems unfair to them. Because they're driven to be the best, they're usually good at whatever interests them, but they can become bored if they're not adequately challenged. They usually come across as confident and self-assured but may also appear somewhat aloof, and they often don't show affection easily. Logical and analytical, Strategic Problem Solvers are often very objective and don't tend to take things personally.

Strategic Problem Solvers represent only about 10% of the population, making them one of the rarest personality types.

How you're similar to and different from your child

In general, the more similar two people's personality types are, the easier the relationship—not necessarily better—but easier. The three components of personality in which people can be most similar or different are the way they perceive the world, their core motivators, and their preferred communication style.

It's probably no surprise that you and your child are quite different. **Responsible Hard Workers** like you take in information primarily through their five senses. They focus on their current reality, on what's happening in the moment, and not on what they imagine might happen sometime in the future. But Strategic Problem Solvers rely heavily on their intuition or sixth sense to take in information, focusing less on what is than what's possible, what something means and how it is connected to other things. They also usually have a vivid imagination.

Another important difference is in what motivates the two of you, which often influences the behaviors and activities that give you your greatest satisfaction. Responsible Hard Workers usually derive their greatest satisfaction from being of service in a real and tangible way, often in a traditional setting in which there are clear expectations. For example, you have encouraged and are very proud of your daughter (who is also a Responsible Hard Worker), who has made a commitment to tutor a younger child in math and meets with her each week.

In contrast, most Strategic Problem Solvers derive their greatest satisfaction from continuing to learn, developing new competencies, and being successful. They are especially gratified when, faced with a new challenge, they can come up with an innovative solution.

Another difference between these two types is what is referred to as their temperaments, which can greatly influence a person's key drives, core values, interests, and specific behaviors. Words that are most commonly used to describe the temperament of Responsible Hard Workers such as you are responsible, dependable, organized, hard-working, productive, and compliant. In contrast, adjectives most used to describe the temperament of your Strategic Problem Solver child are competent, confident, intellectual, independent, high-achieving, and competitive.

Another component is the different ways in which these two types communicate and prefer to be communicated with. Responsible Hard Workers usually like to talk about real things happening in the present that involve practical solutions. Their language tends to be straightforward and includes plenty of details. In contrast, Strategic Problem Solvers like best to discuss big ideas and possibilities that may not even exist. Their language tends to be complex, often involving multiple ideas in the same sentence. As a result of these very different styles, Responsible Hard Workers often find Strategic Problem Solvers unclear and confusing, while Strategic Problem

Solvers often complain that their counterparts get so mired in the details, they fail to see the big picture, nuances, or implications.

How this may play out in your relationship

All parents want what's best for their children. And often, mostly unconsciously, parents believe their children will be happier and more successful by being more like them. But what happens when your child is very different from you?

Many child psychologists believe that the happiest, healthiest children are those whose parents really understand and appreciate them for the unique individuals they are. This is what fosters self-esteem. Of course, the opposite is also true: when children are not seen for who they are or appreciated and celebrated for their gifts, they often grow up not feeling good about themselves—or not good enough, in general.

Responsible Hard Worker parents' priority is to keep their children safe. They tend to be cautious, risk averse, and comfortable practicing long-held, familiar traditions. They tend to see many things as either black or white, while their Strategic Problem Solver children are more likely to see things in various shades of grey. There are many opportunities for these differences to present themselves, from eating dinner at the same time every night to making quite radical choices. As an example, you become upset that your daughter has chosen to participate in a regional science fair rather than attend the yearly family reunion. How the two of you view this situation reflects a difference in priorities, which understanding can help reduce some of the tension.

The days are long gone when people believed that children should be seen and not heard. Parents of Strategic Problem Solvers quickly learn that their children are usually not shy about arguing or expressing their (sometimes very strong) opinions. Although it might not seem like it at the time, they are not doing this to be disrespectful, combative, or disruptive. They simply learn best by questioning, debating, and logically weighing the pros and cons.

Potential vulnerabilities

Although every individual is unique, research shows that Strategic Problem Solvers may have a lower-than-average risk of developing anxiety and depression and may be less susceptible to others' negative online behavior. But every individual is unique. Your child may not necessarily be at increased, or decreased, risk.

How to nurture your child

"Meet your child where they are." Great advice: easy to give, but much harder to do! Stretching outside of your comfort zone is hard and may take some practice, especially when your and your child's personality types are very different. But it is no less important than making sure your child is safe, clothed, or fed, and it may be even more critical to protecting their mental health and promoting their wellbeing.

We all have gifts that make us special, for which we want and need to be appreciated. As a Responsible Hard Worker, among the things you probably value most about yourself are your consistency, reliability, and strong work ethic. But your Strategic Problem Solver has very different gifts: a quick and agile mind, intellectual curiosity, and the ability to be logical and objective and to quickly grasp complex ideas and concepts. Recognizing and appreciating these gifts lets your child know that you see and love them for who they are, especially if they are very different from you.

A special word to Responsible Hard Worker parents: by your nature, you tend to be fairly conservative, conventional, and comfortable doing things the way they're usually done. But most Strategic Problem Solver children are very different: they are energized and excited by learning and trying new ideas and generally more comfortable embracing change. Understanding and appreciating these qualities can help you increase your child's self-esteem and confidence.

Because Strategic Problem Solver children tend to be logical and analytical, they often don't know how they feel about things; even if they do know, they may not be comfortable discussing those feelings. As for the parents, there are two types of Responsible Hard Workers: Feelers and Thinkers. Feelers are more sensitive and generally more in tune with their own and others' feelings. Thinkers are more logical and analytical and generally less equipped and less comfortable dealing with emotional issues. But all children of Feelers and Thinkers alike are emotionally vulnerable and need their parents to be able to help them understand and deal with what they are feeling. Feeling Responsible Hard Worker parents may be more effective in this arena, but in some cases the child may relate better to the parent who is the Thinker, because all Strategic Problem Solvers are also Thinkers.

Your Strategic Problem Solver child probably has a rich imagination and enjoys using it. Asking them to brainstorm solutions to a problem they present to you is more likely to get them engaged, and, as a bonus, you're likely to learn more about what's going on in their life, as well.

With that said, here are:

Tried and true suggestions for engaging your
Strategic Problem Solver:

- Compliment them on their creative ideas and logical arguments and be willing to let them win.
- Model open and honest communication of feelings; help them develop kindness, generosity, and tact.
- Expect to be challenged and respect their strong need for independence.
- Be fair and consistent in discipline; explain the logical, rational reasons for decisions and rules.
- Try not to take a lack of overt affection on their part personally and find common interests to foster closeness and intimacy.
- Reward them with increasing levels of responsibility and praise them for their accomplishments.

This information is provided for educational purposes only and is not meant to diagnose any condition, or explain or predict any future behavior or conditions in children or adults of any personality type, as each person is a unique individual.

CHAPTER 7
Responsible Hard Worker Parent (Type 1) & Adventurous Free Spirit Child (Type 3)

Of course, you know your child better than anyone! But with some types of children, regardless of how diligent the parent is, it's almost impossible to know what's going on beneath the surface. This Parent/Child Profile provides important new insights into your child, yourself, and how your similarities and differences affect your interactions, all with an eye toward helping you build the healthiest, most fulfilling relationship possible.

Your personality type:

Responsible Hard Worker
Always trying to do the right thing.

Responsible Hard Workers tend to be serious and cautious. They like familiar routines and traditions. By their nature, they like structure, boundaries, and following the rules, and they expect others to follow them, too.

Responsible Hard Workers usually respect authority figures such as parents, teachers, doctors, and police officers and tend not to push the envelope or rock the boat. As team players, they have a strong sense of duty and often feel an obligation to help others and to be of service. They often volunteer for service clubs or religious houses of worship. They are planners who can become annoyed when plans are changed, especially at the last minute. Their word is their bond. They have a strong work ethic and pride themselves on finishing whatever they start. They often make to-do lists and like to check off completed tasks.

One finds Responsible Hard Workers in all occupations, but they often gravitate to work that is fairly structured, provides clear instructions and expectations, and encourages and rewards them for working hard and meeting their employer's goals. Specific fields that attract many people of this type include management, the law, business, law enforcement, teaching, operations, finance, healthcare, engineering, and computer science.

Responsible Hard Workers represent about 46% of the population, making them the most common personality type.

Your child's personality type:

Adventurous Free Spirit
Seize the day!

Adventurous Free Spirits love to have fun and tend to not take things too seriously. Rather than make plans in advance, they prefer to be spontaneous and respond to whatever is happening in the moment. As a result, they can be impulsive and take more risks than their parents are comfortable with. Adventurous Free Spirit children learn best by doing, rather than by reading or listening to a lecture. The more physical and tactile the experience, the more lasting impression it will leave on this type of child.

Many Adventurous Free Spirits are naturally competitive, like to win, and tend to not be especially concerned about how the person they defeat may feel about their loss. Most of these kids are quite physical, enjoying sports and being in nature. They also may like to take things apart to see how they work—and can usually figure out how to put them back together again. These are kids who don't like being told what to do and are likely to bend the rules whenever they think they can get away with it. These children can also be impulsive and do things that seemed like a good idea…at the time.

Adventurous Free Spirits represent about 18% of the population.

How you're similar to and different from your child

In general, the more similar two people's personality types, the easier the relationship. Not necessarily better, but easier. The three components of personality in which people can be most similar or different are the way they perceive the world, their core motivators, and their preferred communication style.

It's probably no surprise that you and your child are quite different. A happy coincidence and helpful dynamic about your two types is that **Responsible Hard Workers** and **Adventurous Free**

Spirits both take in information primarily through their five senses. They focus on their current reality, what's happening in the moment, and not on what they imagine might happen sometime in the future. This usually leads them to understand the world in much the same way.

Another important difference is in what motivates the two of you, which often influences the behaviors and activities that give you your greatest satisfaction. Most Responsible Hard Workers derive their greatest satisfaction from working hard, being of service in a real and tangible way, often in a traditional setting in which they can use their skills to meet their employer's objectives. For example, you may find volunteer work through a church, temple, mosque, or service organization fulfilling.

In contrast, most Adventurous Free Spirits derive their greatest satisfaction from living in the moment and enjoying their lives with as few rules and people telling them what to do as possible. They usually have a much more casual, playful demeanor, embracing a "don't worry, be happy" approach to life. As an example, your son may choose to take easier high school courses, which will allow him to spend his senior year playing football—a game he loves. However, you worry that decision may affect his getting into his first-choice college. This represents a fundamental clash of values, as you believe working hard to achieve his long-term goal should be his top priority.

One of the most significant differences between these two types are their temperaments, innate qualities that influence a person's values and key motivators. Adjectives often used to describe the Responsible Hard Worker's temperament are dependable, organized, productive, service-oriented, trustworthy, traditional, and consistent. In contrast, words that best describe Adventurous Free Spirits are fun-loving, risk taking, spontaneous, active, adaptable, and impulsive.

Another component of your relationship is the different ways your two types communicate and prefer to be communicated with. Responsible Hard Workers usually like to talk about real things happening in the present and focus on practical solutions to problems. Their language tends to be straightforward and include plenty of details. They tend to communicate efficiently and don't waste time going off on irrelevant tangents. Adventurous Free Spirits' communication style also tends to be simple and straightforward, but it can be more casual, and it may take them a little longer to get to the point, even when the subject at hand may require some urgency.

How this may play out in your relationship

All parents want what's best for their kids. Often, mostly unconsciously, parents believe their children will be happier and more successful by being more like them. But what happens when your child is very different from you?

Many child psychologists believe that the happiest, healthiest children are those whose parents really understand and appreciate them for the unique individuals they are. This is what fosters self-esteem. Of course, the opposite is also true: when children are not seen for who they are, or appreciated and celebrated for their gifts, they often grow up not feeling good about themselves—or not good enough, in general.

Responsible Hard Workers tend to be cautious and are typically not risk takers. But most Adventurous Free Spirit children are just the opposite. They feel most alive when they're pushing their physical limits, which often involves taking risks. Parents of these children have a delicate balancing act: they need to allow their child to experience the world the way they are naturally hardwired to do (which might make the parent uncomfortable) while at the same time keeping them safe.

Responsible Hard Workers tend to have a strong work ethic, are driven to complete what they start, and seldom procrastinate. Their word is their bond: simply put, they do what they say they will do and expect their children to as well. But Adventurous Free Spirit children enjoy whatever they're doing in the moment and tend to have more of a "play ethic." This means they may be inclined to drop what they're doing (especially if it's an arduous task) if some fun opportunity presents itself. This doesn't mean they don't get their tasks completed, only that it may take a while. In addition, Responsible Hard Worker parents tend to be organized and prefer to run a tight ship. Because their Adventurous Free Spirit child has a more casual, laid-back approach to life, many Responsible Hard Worker parents also struggle with their Adventurous Free Spirit child around getting them to get up and go to bed on time, finishing homework or projects when they're due, or keeping their room neat.

Finally, Responsible Hard Workers tend to have traditional

values and especially enjoy maintaining long-held family traditions. This is especially true for Feeling Responsible Hard Workers, who tend to be more sensitive and relationship-oriented than their Thinking counterparts, who are more logical and analytical and less sentimental. However, Adventurous Free Spirit children often don't share the same needs as their parents. For example, a Responsible Hard Worker parent gets upset with his son when his son opts out of going to a rarely held family reunion because he wants to go skiing with his best friend and his family.

Potential vulnerabilities

Research shows that Adventurous Free Spirits may have a slightly higher-than-average risk for anxiety and depression and may also be more affected by online bullying. But not all Adventurous Free Spirits are created equally, so some may be at even greater risk than others. However, because every individual is unique, your child may not necessarily be at increased or decreased risk.

How to nurture your child

"Meet your child where they are." Great advice: easy to give, but much harder to do! Stretching outside of your comfort zone is hard and may take some practice, especially when your and your child's personality types are very different. But it is no less important than making sure your child is safe, clothed, or fed, and it may be critical to protecting their mental health and promoting their wellbeing.

We all have gifts that make us special and for which we want and need to be appreciated. As a Responsible Hard Worker, among the things you probably value most about yourself are your consistency, reliability, desire to always do the right thing, and strong work ethic. Your Adventurous Free Spirit child's greatest gifts are likely very different. They are keen observers of what's happening around them, quick to act, often good at getting others engaged, and usually good in a crisis. Recognizing and appreciating their gifts lets your child know that you see and love them for who they are, especially if they are very different from you.

As mentioned earlier, Responsible Hard Worker parents who are Thinkers tend not be especially tuned into feelings, either their child's or their own. They may also find conversations that deal with emotions difficult and out of their comfort zone. Many Adventurous Free Spirit children are also not naturally especially in tune with their feelings and may be uncomfortable sharing them. A parent who is a Feeler may have an easier time gently coaxing their child to open up to them.

When trying to engage your Adventurous Free Spirit child in a conversation, they are more likely to respond to specific questions rooted in reality rather than hypothetical ones that require them to use their imagination. For example, if you ask them "What do you think Jason will do if you tell him he hurt your feelings?" you're likely to be met with a blank stare, followed by "I don't know." (Because they don't.) But if you ask them "Have you told Jason that he hurt your feelings?" followed by "What did he say (or do)?" you'll have a better chance of getting them to provide additional information that will help you have a more productive conversation.

With that said, here are:

Tried and true suggestions for engaging your Adventurous Free Spirit:

- Use fun activities and treats to reward positive behavior; turn chores into games and make them fun whenever possible.
- Recognize that they learn best by experiencing things first-hand.
- Teach them how to take reasonable risks, steering them toward activities that excite, but aren't like to injure, them.
- Don't misinterpret a lack of overt affection as a lack of love and caring.
- Set crystal-clear boundaries, and show them what you mean, rather than simply telling them.

This information is provided for educational purposes only and is not meant to diagnose any condition, or explain or predict any future behavior or conditions in children or adults of any personality type, as each person is a unique individual.

CHAPTER 8
Responsible Hard Worker Parent (Type 1) & Gentle Humble Helper Child (Type 4)

Of course, you know your child better than anyone! But with some types of children, regardless of how diligent the parent is, it's almost impossible to know what's going on beneath the surface. This Parent/Child Profile provides important new insights into your child, yourself, and how your similarities and differences affect your interactions, all with an eye toward helping you build the healthiest, most fulfilling relationship possible.

Your personality type:

Responsible Hard Worker
Always trying to do the right thing.

Responsible Hard Workers tend to be serious and cautious. They like familiar routines and traditions. By their nature, they like structure, boundaries, and following the rules, and they expect others to follow them, too.

Responsible Hard Workers usually respect authority figures such as parents, teachers, doctors, and police officers and tend not to push the envelope or rock the boat. As team players, they have a strong sense of duty and often feel an obligation to help others and to be of service. They often volunteer for service clubs or religious houses of worship. They are planners who can become annoyed when plans are changed, especially at the last minute. Their word is their bond. They have a strong work ethic and pride themselves on finishing whatever they start. They often make to-do lists and like to check off completed tasks.

One finds Responsible Hard Workers in all occupations, but

they often gravitate to work that is fairly structured, provides clear instructions and expectations, and encourages and rewards them for working hard and meeting their employer's goals. Specific fields that attract many people of this type include management, the law, business, law enforcement, teaching, operations, finance, healthcare, engineering, and computer science.

Responsible Hard Workers represent about 46% of the population, making them the most common personality type.

Your child's personality type:

Gentile Humble Helper
Practice Random Acts of Kindness.

Gentle Humble Helpers tend to be easy-going, warm, kind-hearted, and modest. They are very sensitive and feel things deeply but are likely to share their feelings only with people they trust. These are kids who like to please others and avoid conflict at all costs. They are usually very loyal friends who are good at sharing their toys and possessions.

Gentle Humble Helpers are natural nurturers. They usually get great pleasure from helping others, especially younger children, and are often drawn to and fond of caring for animals. These are fairly realistic kids, and so their play often tends to be more physical, like participating in sports, climbing trees, and playing hide-and-seek, rather than engaging in word games or making up imaginary scenarios.

Gentle Humble Helpers usually have a good sense of humor, but if they make jokes, it is seldom at anyone else's expense. They like being spontaneous and responding to what comes up rather than making plans for the future. They can also be impulsive, doing things that seem like a good idea…at the time.

Gentle Humble Helpers represent only about 9% of the population, making them the rarest of the five personality types.

How you're similar to and different from your child

In general, the more similar two people's personality types, the easier the relationship. Not necessarily better, but easier. The three components of personality in which people can be most similar or different are the way they perceive the world, their core motivators, and their preferred communication style.

It's probably no surprise that you and your child are quite different. A happy coincidence and helpful dynamic about your two types is that Responsible Hard Workers and Gentle Humble Helpers both take in information primarily through their five senses, perceiving the world in a similar way. They tend to focus on their current reality, what's happening in the moment, and not on what they imagine might happen sometime in the future. This usually leads parents and children of these two types to understand the world in much the same way.

Another important difference is in what motivates the two of you, which often influences the behaviors and activities that give you your greatest satisfaction. Most Responsible Hard Worker parents derive their greatest satisfaction from working hard, being of service in real and tangible ways, preferably in a traditional setting in which they can use their skills to meet their employer's objectives.

In contrast, most Gentle Humble Helpers derive their greatest satisfaction from helping others, living in the moment, and enjoying their lives with as few rules and people telling them what to do as possible. Although they tend to be casual and have a playful demeanor, these are children who feel things very deeply. As an example, your child may have a habit of bringing home stray cats or dogs, or as a young child may be inconsolable if they witness another person or animal being treated badly.

For several reasons, Responsible Hard Workers moms are often—but not always—more comfortable dealing with emotions than dads of the same type. This is important to keep in mind because Gentle Humble Helpers need a very gentle touch, especially when dealing with sensitive subjects.

One of the most significant differences between these two types is their temperament, the innate qualities that influence a person's values and key motivators. Adjectives often used to describe the Responsible Hard Worker's temperament are dependable, organized, productive, service-oriented, trustworthy, traditional, and consistent. In contrast, Gentle Humble Helpers are most often described as being sensitive, fun-loving, humble, nurturing, adaptable, helpful, and cooperative.

Another component in your relationship is the different ways these two types communicate and prefer to be communicated with. Responsible Hard Workers usually like to talk about real things happening in the present and are good at coming up with practical solutions to problems. Their language tends to be straightforward and include plenty of details. They usually communicate efficiently and don't waste time going off on irrelevant tangents. Gentle Humble Helpers' communication style also tends to be simple and straightforward, but the things they like to talk about more often reflect some personal experience and how they and others felt about it. They are also more likely to use language that reflects their values, making statements like "I loved that." "It was terrible." Or "She was so wonderful!"

How this may play out in your relationship

All parents want what's best for their kids. Often, mostly unconsciously, parents believe their children will be happier and more successful by being more like them. But what happens when your child is very different from you?

Many child psychologists believe that the happiest, healthiest children are those whose parents really understand and appreciate them for the unique individuals they are. This is what fosters self-esteem. Of course, the opposite is also true: when children are not seen for who they are or appreciated and celebrated for their gifts, they often grow up not feeling good about themselves—or not good enough, in general.

Responsible Hard Worker parents' priority is to keep their children safe. They tend to be cautious; they are not natural risk-takers. But most Gentle Humble Helper children are comfortable taking risks and tend to be impulsive, sometimes acting before they've really thought things through.

But experiencing things fully, especially physically, is how Gentle Humble Helpers learn best and is what brings them the greatest joy. So, the challenge for parents of these types of children is to let them take calculated risks while keeping them safe.

Responsible Hard Workers tend to have a strong work ethic, are driven to complete what they start, and seldom procrastinate. Their word is their bond: simply put, they do what they say they will do and expect their children to as well. But Gentle Humble Helpers tend to enjoy whatever they're doing in the moment and tend to have more of a "play ethic." This means they may be inclined to drop what they're doing (especially if it's an arduous task) if some fun opportunity presents itself. This doesn't mean they don't get their tasks completed, only that it may take a while.

Potential vulnerabilities

Research shows that Gentle Humble Helpers have a higher-than-average risk of developing anxiety and depression and may be more susceptible to bullying and others' negative online behavior. But because every individual is unique, this does not mean that your child is necessarily at increased, or decreased, risk.

How to nurture your child

"Meet your child where they are." Great advice: easy to give, and much harder to do! Stretching outside of one's comfort zone is hard and may take some practice, especially when the parent's and child's personality types are very different. But it is no less important than making sure your child is safe, clothed, or fed and may be more critical to protecting their mental health and promoting their wellbeing.

We all have gifts that make us special and for which we want and need to be appreciated. As a Responsible Hard Worker, among the things you probably value most about yourself are your consistency, reliability, and strong work ethic. But your Gentle Humble Helper's greatest gift is likely their desire and ability to be a helpful, loyal friend. Recognizing and appreciating your child's greatest gifts lets them know that you see and love them for who they are.

Some Responsible Hard Worker parents, called Thinkers, are naturally more logical and analytical than others. It's important for these parents to remember how sensitive their child is, and they may need to stretch out of their comfort zone to meet their child where they are.

Other Responsible Hard Worker parents, called Feelers, are more naturally sensitive and tuned in to people's emotions. While Feeling Responsible Hard Worker parents are more generally more comfortable and agile in dealing with their child's feelings, they may avoid having difficult conversations for fear of upsetting their child.

When trying to engage your Gentle Humble Helper child in a conversation, they are more likely to respond to specific questions rooted in reality rather than hypothetical ones that require them to use their imagination. For example, if you ask them "What do you think Jason will do if you tell him he hurt your feelings?" you're likely to be met with a blank stare, followed by "I don't know." (Because they don't.) But if you ask them "Have you told Jason that he hurt your feelings?" followed by "What did he say (or do)?" you'll have a better chance of getting them to provide additional information that will help you have a more productive conversation.

Tried and true suggestions for engaging your
Gentle Humble Helper:

- Smile, give them lots of hugs and kisses, and frequently tell them you love them.
- Give them very specific directions and instructions and show them what you mean whenever possible.
- Accept their need to be physically active. Play with them and surprise them; be spontaneous.
- Support their feelings and allow them to express them in their own time and style.
- Use incentives and rewards that are tangible, such as fun activities, freedom, money, and treats.

This information is provided for educational purposes only and is not meant to diagnose any condition, or explain or predict any future behavior or conditions in children or adults of any personality type, as each person is a unique individual.

CHAPTER 9
Responsible Hard Worker Parent (Type 1) & Creative Sensitive Soul Child (Type 5)

Of course, you know your child better than anyone! But with some types of children, regardless of how diligent the parent, it's almost impossible to know what's going on beneath the surface. This Parent/Child Profile provides important new insights into your child, yourself, and how your similarities and differences affect your interactions, all with an eye toward helping you build the healthiest, most fulfilling relationship possible.

Your personality type:

Responsible Hard Worker
Always trying to do the right thing.

Responsible Hard Workers tend to be serious and cautious. They like familiar routines and traditions. By their nature, they like structure, boundaries, and following the rules, and they expect others to follow them, too.

Responsible Hard Workers usually respect authority figures such as parents, teachers, doctors, and police officers and tend not to push the envelope or rock the boat. As team players, they have a strong sense of duty and often feel an obligation to help others and to be of service. They often volunteer for service clubs or religious houses of worship. They are planners who can become annoyed when plans are changed, especially at the last minute. Their word is their bond. They have a strong work ethic and pride themselves on finishing whatever they start. They often make to-do lists and like to check off completed tasks.

One finds Responsible Hard Workers in all occupations, but

they often gravitate to work that is fairly structured, provides clear instructions and expectations, and encourages and rewards them for working hard and meeting their employer's goals. Specific fields that attract many people of this type include management, the law, business, law enforcement, teaching, operations, finance, healthcare, engineering, and computer science.

Responsible Hard Workers represent about 46% of the population, making them the most common personality type.

Your child's personality type:

Creative Sensitive Soul
Seeing possibilities everywhere.

Creative Sensitive Souls feel things deeply and are very empathetic. As a result, they avoid conflict and try to make people happy, often putting others' needs ahead of themselves. Because these children often feel things more intensely than other types of children, they can feel lonely and sometimes sense that they don't quite belong.

Because Creative Sensitive Souls have vivid imaginations and feel things so deeply, they are the most idealistic of all the types. They know the way things should be (but seldom are), which can cause them to become moody, disillusioned, or depressed. Usually loving and physically affectionate, they may also be easily frightened and prone to worrying.

Many Creative Sensitive Souls are, as their name implies, creative, which they may express through art, music, poetry, dance, acting, and other such endeavors. They often have vivid imaginations, and when they're young they may like to play games that begin with "Let's pretend..." They tend to take things personally and can be moody and easily upset when criticized.

Creative Sensitive Souls represent about 17% of the population.

How you're similar to and different from your child

In general, the more similar two people's personality types, the easier, though not necessarily better, the relationship. Three similarities and differences have the greatest impact: how people perceive the world, their core motivators, and their preferred communication style.

It's probably no surprise that you and your child are quite dif ferent. Responsible Hard Workers take in information primarily through their five senses. They focus on their current reality, what's happening in the moment, and not on what they imagine might happen sometime in the future. For example, your high school senior is filling out college applications but has no idea what he might want to study or which career path he might want to pursue.

But Creative Sensitive Souls rely heavily on their intuition or sixth sense to take in information, focusing less on what is than what is possible, what something means and how it is connected to other things. Another way to look at this is that while Responsible Hard Workers focus on the details and specifics, Creative Sensitive Souls prefer to look at the big picture and can easily connect the dots.

Another important difference is in what motivates the two of you, a factor that often influences the behaviors and activities that give you your greatest satisfaction. Responsible Hard Workers such as you usually derive their greatest satisfaction from being of service in a real and tangible way, often in a traditional setting in which there are clear expectations. For example, you've encouraged and are very proud of your daughter who has made a commitment to tutor a younger child in math and meets with her weekly.

In contrast, most Creative Sensitive Souls value most about themselves their authenticity and ability to create and nurture meaningful, harmonious relationships. Many Creative Sensitive Souls are drawn to causes and work tirelessly to right a wrong or try to improve other peoples' lives. This is true even for children of this type. For example, even though he is only ten years old, your son has heard about a homeless family and has become obsessed with raising money to help them—an activity you are likely to wholeheartedly support.

These two personality types also have different temperaments, often considered the core of one's personality type, that influence their values, competencies, and interests. Some words most used to describe Responsible Hard Workers are trustworthy, reliable, dependable, organized, hard-working, and productive. Adjectives that describe most Creative Sensitive Souls are empathetic, idealist, perceptive, creative, spiritual, compassionate, and collaborative.

Another component is the different ways these two types communicate and prefer to be communicated with. Responsible Hard Workers usually like to talk about real things happening in the present that involve practical solutions. Their language tends to be straightforward and usually includes plenty of details. But since empathy is a key characteristic of Creative Sensitive Souls like your child, they're usually most interested in talking about people, what they're experiencing now or may experience in the future, and, if a person is struggling, how they can help them. Creative Sensitive Souls' language tends to be complicated, often stringing several thoughts together in the same sentence. And because many love language, they usually have a sophisticated vocabulary. Because of these differences, Creative Sensitive Souls can sometimes find Responsible Hard Workers a little boring and think they include way too many details, while Responsible Hard Workers can find Creative Sensitive Souls unclear, confusing, and unfocused.

How this may play out in your relationship

All parents want what's best for their kids. Often, mostly unconsciously, parents believe their children will be happier and more successful by being more like them. But what happens when your child is very different from you?

Many child psychologists believe that the happiest, healthiest children are those whose parents really understand and appreciate them for the unique individuals they are. This is what fosters self-esteem. Of course, the opposite is also true: when children are not seen for who they are or appreciated and celebrated for their gifts, they often grow up not feeling good about themselves—or not good enough, in general.

Responsible Hard Worker parents tend to be quite conservative. They are by nature people who respect authority, follow rules, and don't usually color outside the lines or rock the boat. They tend to be creatures of habit and like doing things the way they've always done them. For example, they often place high value on the importance of maintaining traditions and routines such as eating dinner as a family together every night at the same time.

Creative Sensitive Souls are often quite different. They're creative, like to think outside the box, and are drawn to and usually embrace new, alternative, and perhaps unusual ideas. It's not uncommon for Responsible Hard Worker parents to be, at least initially, skeptical about a new idea their child comes up with and, to help their child succeed, make suggestions based on their more practical minds. Though well intentioned, these behaviors can make Creative Sensitive Soul children feel that their creativity is being stifled and not appreciated.

Potential vulnerabilities

Research shows that Creative Sensitive Souls may be at significantly higher risk for anxiety and depression and may also be more affected by bullying, both in person and online. But not all Creative Sensitive Souls are created equal, so some may be at greater risk than others. However, because every individual is unique, your child may not necessarily be at increased or decreased risk.

How to nurture your child

"Meet your child where they are." Great advice: easy to give, and much harder to do! Stretching outside of one's comfort zone is hard and may take some practice, especially when the parent's and child's personality types are very different. But it is no less important than making sure your child is safe, clothed, or fed and may be more critical to protecting their mental health and promoting their wellbeing.

We all have gifts that make us special and for which we want and need to be appreciated. As a Responsible Hard Worker, among the things you probably value most about yourself are your consistency, reliability, and strong work ethic. But your Creative Sensitive Soul's greatest gift is likely their empathy and desire to make a positive difference in others' lives. Recognizing and appreciating your child's greatest gifts lets them know that you see and love them for who they are.

Remember that Creative Sensitive Souls are extremely sensitive but often have a hard time sharing their feelings. It's not unusual for one parent to naturally be better at having conversations that involve emotions. If this is the case, the other parent can learn to communicate more effectively by watching and listening to how that parent interacts with their child.

There are actually two varieties of Responsible Hard Worker parents. Some, called Thinkers, are naturally more logical and analytical. For these parents, it's important to remember how sensitive their child is, and they may need to stretch out of their comfort zone to meet their child where they are at.

Other Responsible Hard Worker parents, called Feelers, are more naturally sensitive and tuned in to others' emotions. While

Feeling Responsible Hard Worker parents are generally more comfortable dealing with their child's feelings, they may avoid having difficult conversations for fear of upsetting their child.

Your Creative Sensitive Soul child probably has and enjoys using a rich imagination. Asking them to brainstorm solutions to a problem they share with you (especially if they're more extraverted) is more likely to get them engaged, and you're likely to learn more about what's going on in their life, as well.

With that said, here are:

Tried and true suggestions for engaging your
Creative Sensitive Soul:

- Try not to judge or rush them through their feelings.
- Appreciate their individuality and express your love and affection frequently.
- Forgive them quickly and never give them the silent treatment.
- Encourage them to speak their truth and not feel they have to sugarcoat things.
- Listen to and support their ideas; don't squelch their creativity or originality.

This information is provided for educational purposes only and is not meant to diagnose any condition, or explain or predict any future behavior or conditions in children or adults of any personality type, as each person is a unique individual.

Strategic Problem Solver Parent

and their Child Personality Types

CHAPTER 10
Strategic Problem Solver Parent (Type 2) & Responsible Hard Worker Child (Type 1)

Of course, you know your child better than anyone! But with some types of children, regardless of how diligent the parent, it's almost impossible to know what's going on beneath the surface. This Parent/Child Profile provides important new insights into your child, yourself, and how your similarities and differences affect your interactions, all with an eye toward helping you build the healthiest, most fulfilling relationship possible.

Your personality type:

Strategic Problem Solver
Everything can be improved.

Strategic Problem Solvers tend to be independent, strong-willed, and competitive. Their love of learning drives them to excel and often results in their being over-achievers. Their thought processes can be complex; they connect the dots quite easily and are usually gifted at seeing how things can be improved.

Strategic Problem Solvers may be challenging to interact with because they often like to argue or push back, especially when something doesn't make sense or seem fair to them. Because they're driven to be the best, they set high standards for themselves and others. They usually come across as confident and self-assured, but they may also appear somewhat aloof and often don't show affection easily.

One finds Strategic Problem Solvers in all occupations, but they often gravitate to work that allows them to be independent, continue to learn, solve problems creatively, advance in the organization,

and be recognized and well compensated for their competence. A high percentage of them are found in leadership positions. Specific fields that often attract this type include college-level teaching, research, law, technology, economics and finance, science, psychiatry, architecture, and consulting.

Strategic Problem Solvers represent only about 10% of the population, making them one of the rarest personality types.

Your child's personality type:

Responsible Hard Worker
Always trying to do the right thing.

Responsible Hard Workers tend to be serious and cautious. They like familiar routines and traditions. By their nature, they like structure and boundaries and tend to follow the rules, and they expect others to follow them, too.

As children and adolescents, Responsible Hard Workers are usually not especially challenging to parent. They tend to be fairly compliant when it comes to doing their chores, finishing their homework, and helping out with younger siblings. They usually take their responsibilities, such as caring for their pets, seriously.

Responsible Hard Workers usually respect authority figures such as parents, teachers, doctors, and police officers, and they don't tend to push the envelope or rock the boat. They have a strong sense of duty and often feel an obligation to help others. They're most comfortable when plans have been made and can get upset when plans are changed, especially at the last minute. They are usually driven to finish whatever they start, such as games, art projects, or puzzles.

Responsible Hard Workers represent about 46% of the population, making them the most common personality type.

How you're similar to and different from your child

In general, the more similar two people's personality types are, the easier the relationship—not necessarily better—but easier. The three components of personality where people can be most similar or different are: the way they perceive the world, their core motivators, and their preferred communication style.

It's probably no surprise to you that you and your child are quite different from one another; you are hard-wired to see the world in very different ways.

Responsible Hard Worker children like yours take in information primarily through their five senses. They pay attention to what is happening in the moment, not what might happen sometime in the future. For example, your child decides to take an easier course so they can play sports, not factoring in how this might affect their chances of getting into their first-choice college next year.

Strategic Problem Solvers like you operate very differently. You rely heavily on your sixth sense to take in information, focusing less on what is than why it is and how it is connected to other things. People of your type also tend to think more about future possibilities than present realities. The difference in how your two types perceive can often lead to huge misunderstandings and explain why they don't always appreciate the other's point of view.

Another important difference is in your varying motivators, which often determine the behaviors and activities that give you the greatest satisfaction. The key motivator for most **Strategic Problem Solvers** is being successful, which they achieve by being lifelong learners and constantly challenging themselves. **Responsible Hard Workers**, on the other hand, derive their greatest satisfaction from dealing with real things, not ideas or concepts, and from understanding what they need to do, then doing it, usually in a structured way. As an example, your child really loves working on cars and wants to be a mechanic. But you worry that by choosing this line of work, they may not find it intellectually challenging enough or allow them to make a good enough living.

Another difference between these two types is what are referred to as your temperaments, which can greatly influence a person's key drives, core values, interests, and specific behaviors. Words that are most commonly used to describe your **Responsible Hard Worker** child's temperament are responsible, dependable, organized, hard-working, productive, and compliant. In contrast, adjectives most used to describe the temperament of **Strategic Problem Solvers** like you are competent, confident, intellectual, independent, high achiever, and competitive.

Yet another component is the very different ways your two types communicate and prefer to be communicated with. **Responsible Hard Workers** tend to be straightforward and concise and usually talk about real things or situations that are happening in the moment. They can become confused by their **Strategic Problem Solver** parent's desire to talk more about ideas, which can be quite abstract. Strategic Problem Solvers parents can become impatient when their child does not seem to "get it" quickly enough.

How this may play out in your relationship

All parents want what's best for their kids. Often, mostly unconsciously, parents believe their children will be happier and more successful by being more like them. But what happens when your child is very different from you?

Many child psychologists believe that the happiest, healthiest children are those whose parents really understand and appreciate them for the unique individuals they are. This is what fosters self-esteem. Of course, the opposite is also true: when children are not seen for who they are or appreciated and celebrated for their gifts, they often grow up not feeling good about themselves—or not good enough, in general.

Strategic Problem Solvers tend to be high (some would say "over") achievers and usually set very high standards for themselves and others—especially their children. But your Responsible Hard Worker child is simply not hard-wired like you and likely lacks your natural gifts of creativity, analytical thinking, and ambition. Fortunately, they have their own considerable gifts. Sometimes the parent's standards may be impossible to reach, no matter how hard the child tries. Strategic Problem Solvers typically place a high value on academic success, which usually means completing college and perhaps obtaining an advanced degree. But their more practical, down-to-earth Responsible Hard Worker child's idea of success might be acquiring a steady, secure job that pays them a sufficient wage to live on. Unless the parent understands what's most important to their child, they can inadvertently convey their disapproval or disappointment, which might breed disappointment and lead to a lack of self-esteem in their child.

For the logical Strategic Problem Solver, feelings are valid—if they make sense. For example, if their Responsible Hard Worker child were to get bullied, the parent would understand why he is sad. But if their child who is more of Feeler is upset because he wasn't invited to the birthday party of a classmate, one whom they don't really like all that much, that same parent may not understand that their child still feels rejected and may try to talk them out of their feelings.

A word about kids who are more extraverted (you can tell because they're usually more talkative and high energy) or introverted (they're usually quieter and more private): If your child is more extraverted, they'll probably be more comfortable discussing these issues, because extraverts tend to think out loud. If you don't know what an extravert's thinking, you haven't been listening—because they'll tell you! But if you don't know what an introvert's thinking, you haven't asked —or waited long enough for an answer. This is because introverts like to think about things before sharing. Sometimes, it might take them just a few moments to respond, other times, much longer! If your child is more introverted (and especially if you are not!), you need to be very patient and give them time to process things the way they need to.

How to nurture your child

"Meet your child where they are." Great advice: easy to give, and much harder to do! Stretching outside of one's comfort zone is hard and may take some practice, especially when the parent's and child's personality types are very different. But it is no less important than making sure your child is safe, clothed, or fed and may be more critical to protecting their mental health and promoting their wellbeing.

We all have gifts that make us special, things for which we desperately want to be appreciated. As a Strategic Problem Solver, you're justifiably proud of your creativity and ability to easily see how things can be improved. But your Responsible Hard Worker child's greatest gift is their strong work ethic and the fact that they can be counted on to do whatever they say they will.do. Recognizing and appreciating your child's greatest gifts lets them know that you see and love them for who they are.

There are actually two types of Responsible Hard Worker children, Feelers and Thinkers. Feelers are considerably more sensitive and in tune with their own and others' feelings. Thinkers are more logical and analytical and generally less equipped for and less comfortable dealing with emotional issues. But all children are emotionally vulnerable and need their parents to be able to help them understand and deal with what they are feeling. That said, ALL Strategic Problem Solvers are Thinkers. If your child is like you and is also a Thinker, your conversations around emotional issues may be more comfortable for the two of you but not be as helpful for your child. The reality is that all children, even those who appear to have the thickest skins, need help understanding and processing their feelings, especially the scary ones, like fear.

You may find having emotional conversations difficult and out of your comfort zone. But try to frame doing this as a challenge to embrace, because it can have such a huge impact on your child's mental health and wellbeing and bring the two of you closer together.

If your child is more of a Feeling type, the other parent may be more effective in this arena. If this is the case, you may benefit from letting the other parent take the lead and learn from observing them.

When trying to engage your Responsible Hard Worker child in a conversation, they are more likely to respond to specific questions, rooted in reality, rather than hypothetical ones that require them to use their imagination. For example, if you ask them "What do you think Jason will do if you tell him he hurt your feelings?" you're likely to be met with a blank stare, followed by "I don't know." (Because they don't.) But if you ask them "Have you told Jason that he hurt your feelings?" followed by "What did he say (or do)?," you'll have a better chance of getting them to provide additional information that will help you have a more productive conversation.

With that said, here are:

Tried and true suggestions for engaging your
Responsible Hard Worker:

- Be clear and explicit in your directions and requests; say what you mean and mean what you say.
- Prepare them in advance for new experiences and changes in plans.
- Recognize you both want to be, and often are, right. Learn to back off and to choose your battles.
- Be on time; follow through on all your commitments to them.
- Encourage them to question things rather than always taking things at face value.
- Reward them with increasing levels of responsibility and praise them for their accomplishments.

This information is provided for educational purposes only and is not meant to diagnose any condition, or explain or predict any future behavior or conditions in children or adults of any personality type, as each person is a unique individual.

CHAPTER 11
Strategic Problem Solver Parent & Child (Type 2)

Of course, you know your child better than anyone! But with some types of children, regardless of how diligent the parent is, it's almost impossible to know what's going on beneath the surface. This Parent/Child Profile provides important new insights into your child, yourself, and how your similarities and differences affect your interactions, all with an eye toward helping you build the healthiest, most fulfilling relationship possible.

It's relatively rare for children and parents to share the same personality type, but when they do, the two are usually similar in many ways. Personality is a combination of nature—your inborn personality type—and nurture—everything else you experience in life, the greatest influence being your parents. While you and your child may be kindred spirits in many ways, there will be profound differences between the two of you because every person is a unique individual and because of your different ages, generations, experiences, and, most importantly, who you were parented by.

Here is a snapshot of the personality type you share with your child. If after reading this report you think that you may have misidentified your own or your child's type, you may want to revisit Chapter 4.

Your and your child's personality type:

Strategic Problem Solver
Everything can be improved.

Strategic Problem Solvers tend to be independent, strong-willed, and competitive. Their love of learning drives them to excel and often leads them to be high (some would say over) achievers. Their thought process can be complex; they connect the dots quite easily and are usually gifted at seeing how things can be improved.

Strategic Problem Solvers may be challenging to interact with because they often like to argue or push back, especially when something doesn't make sense or seem fair to them. Because they're driven to be the best, they set high standards for themselves and others. They usually come across as confident and self-assured, but they may also appear somewhat aloof and often don't show affection easily.

In many ways, Strategic Problem Solver parents are grown-up versions of their younger selves. Of course they are more capable, competent, and well-rounded, but their hard wiring, which determines how they see the world and make decisions, is very similar.

One finds Strategic Problem Solvers in all occupations, but they often gravitate to work that allows them to be independent, continue to learn, solve problems creatively, advance in the organization, and be recognized and well compensated for their competence. A high percentage of them are found in leadership positions. Specific fields that often attract this type include college-level teaching, research, law, technology, economics and finance, science, psychiatry, architecture, and consulting.

Strategic Problem Solvers represent only about 10% of the population, making them one of the rarest personality types.

Similarities with your child

In general, the more similar two people's personality types, the easier, though not necessarily better, the relationship. Three similarities and differences have the greatest impact: how people perceive the world, their core motivators, and their preferred communication style. The good news is that both of you take in information in much the same way, relying on your intuition, or sixth sense, which gives you both a global perspective. Rather than focus on what it is, you naturally connect the dots, see the big picture, understand how things are related to one another, and often see how things can be improved.

But when two people of the same type do experience conflict, it's often because they are too similar, having parallel weaknessesand blind spots. Weaknesses are things we know we're not good at, while blind spots are things we are unaware of that cause us to not be as effective as we'd like to be.

You may have noticed that it's not unusual to notice a personal quality or behavior in someone else that annoys you. Often, the reason is that we share that same quality but may not be aware of or able to own it. This can be even more prevalent when two people share the same personality type. It can feel like we're looking in the mirror—and don't necessarily like what we see.

For example, confidence is generally considered a desirable trait. And because most Strategic Problem Solvers pride themselves on their competence, they also usually project great confidence. But confidence taken to its extreme can be perceived as arrogance. So, two Strategic Problem Solvers may find this otherwise valuable strength annoying when exhibited by the other person. Compounding this situation is the fact that Strategic Problem Solvers like to be (and often are) right. And they typically have strong opinions that may not be shared by the other person. For example, if a Strategic Problem Solver child makes an assertion (usually with great conviction!) that the parent knows is not correct, how the parent handles that can make a huge difference in whether the child will feel encouraged to speak their mind or inhibited from doing so.

Strategic Problem Solvers' primary motivation, which often influences their values, is being successful, which they achieve by being lifelong learners and by constantly challenging themselves.

A clear advantage for parents and children who are both Strategic Problem Solvers is that you share the same temperament—the innate characteristics that influence so much of who you are, what you value, and how you act in the world. Adjectives that are most often used to describe people of this temperament are independent, strategic, intellectual, competent, confident, high-achieving, assertive, and competitive.

With a talent for objective analysis and coming up with creative solutions, Strategic Problem Solvers tend not to focus on or prioritize what others are feeling; nor are they particularly comfortable providing emotional support. They also tend to have a pretty thick skin and are usually not overly affected by criticism.

How this may play out in your relationship

All parents want what's best for their children. And often, mostly unconsciously, parents believe their children will be happier and more successful by being more like them.

Many child psychologists believe that the happiest, healthiest children are those whose parents really understand and appreciate them for the unique individuals they are. This is what fosters self-esteem. Of course, the opposite is also true: when children are not seen for who they are or appreciated and celebrated for their gifts, they often grow up not feeling good about themselves—or not good enough, in general.

It's important for parents who share the same type with their child to remember that they may think like you, they may sound like you, they may even look like you—but they are not you. It's easy for some parents to think of their child as a "mini-me," which can be a source of tension.

For example, because you probably have high standards, which you usually meet or exceed, it makes sense that you would expect your child to, as well. But if they're not equally interested or invested in a subject or project, they may not put in the effort necessary to succeed and may end up feeling that they've let you down.

Potential vulnerabilities

Research shows that Strategic Problem Solvers may have a lower-than-average risk of developing anxiety and depression and may be less susceptible to bullying and other negative online behavior by others. But every individual is unique. Therefore, this does not mean that your child is necessarily at increased or decreased risk.

Strategic Problem Solver parents also tend to be competitive and like to win. Since they value this quality in themselves, they naturally want to instill it in their child. These parents don't tend to coddle their children, believing it will result in their not being tough or competitive enough. This behavior can show up in many ways, such as not letting your child win at a game you're playing with them, insisting they excel academically, or criticizing their performance on the soccer field.

For all of Strategic Problem Solvers' many competencies, providing emotional support is generally not at the top of the list, and they may find having conversations that involve emotions outside their comfort zone. But people of all ages and types have emotions and feelings that need to be understood and honored for them to grow into healthy human beings. Since this is such an important role of parenthood, you need to be patient as they struggle to develop this critically important part of their personality. Remember, you yourself have spent decades learning how to process your feelings and develop effective coping mechanisms.

How to nurture your child

"Meet your child where they are." Great advice: easy to give, and much harder to do! Stretching outside of one's comfort zone is hard and may take some practice, especially when the parent's and child's personality types are very different. But it is no less important than making sure your child is safe, clothed, or fed and may be more critical to protecting their mental health and promoting their wellbeing.

We all have gifts that make us special and for which we desperately want to be appreciated. As a Strategic Problem Solver, one of the things you likely value most about yourself is your intelligence. You'd probably consider it a greater compliment to be told you've got a brilliant mind than you're such a sweet, kind person. So this should be the easy part of being the same type as your child: knowing they will always feel good when they're praised for their intelligence. The kicker is, most Strategic Problem Solver parents are not particularly good at handing out compliments or heaping praise on others, including their own children. Why? Because these parents don't need praise as much as some other types, they figure their children don't, either.

Not only has your child not yet learned to navigate the world of emotions, but they, like all children, have not yet fully developed their executive function, located in the frontal lobe of their brain. (Nor will they until about age 30!) This area is crucial for planning, decision-making, and other cognitive processes that enable us to control our thoughts and actions, and this explains why your child will make LOTS of mistakes, which they need to make in order to learn. So, the message to Strategic Problem Solver parents is to be patient, which will yield huge dividends in the future!

Both you and your Strategic Problem Solver child probably have rich imaginations and enjoy using them. Asking your child to help brainstorm solutions to a problem they share with you (especially if they're more extraverted) is more likely to get them engaged, and you're likely to learn more about what's going on in their life, as well.

With that said, here are:

Tried and true suggestions for engaging your Strategic Problem Solver:

- Compliment them on their creative ideas and logical arguments and be willing to let them win.
- Model open and honest communication of feelings; help them develop kindness, generosity, and tact.
- Expect to be challenged and respect their strong need for independence.

- Be fair and consistent in discipline; explain the logical, rational reasons for decisions and rules.
- Try not to take a lack of overt affection on their part personally and find common interests to foster closeness and intimacy.
- Reward them with increasing levels of responsibility and praise them for their accomplishments.

This information is provided for educational purposes only and is not meant to diagnose any condition, or explain or predict any future behavior or conditions in children or adults of any personality type, as each person is a unique individual.

CHAPTER 12
Strategic Problem Solver Parent (Type 2) & Adventurous Free Spirit Child (Type 3)

Of course, you know your child better than anyone! But with some types of children, regardless of how diligent the parent is, it's almost impossible to know what's going on beneath the surface. This Parent/Child Profile provides important new insights into your child, yourself, and how your similarities and differences affect your interactions, all with an eye toward helping you build the healthiest, most fulfilling relationship possible.

Your personality type:

Strategic Problem Solver
Everything can be improved.

Strategic Problem Solvers tend to be independent, strong-willed, and competitive. Their love of learning drives them to excel and often results in their being overachievers. Their thought processes can be complex; they connect the dots quite easily and are usually gifted at seeing how things can be improved.

Strategic Problem Solvers may be challenging to interact with because they often like to argue or push back, especially when something doesn't make sense or seem fair to them. Because they're driven to be the best, they set high standards for themselves and others. They usually come across as confident and self-assured, but they may also appear somewhat aloof and often don't show affection easily.

One finds Strategic Problem Solvers in all occupations, but they often gravitate to work that allows them to be independent, continue to learn, solve problems creatively, advance in the organization,

and be recognized and well compensated for their competence. A high percentage of them are found in leadership positions. Specific fields that often attract this type include college-level teaching, research, law, technology, economics and finance, science, psychiatry, architecture, and consulting.

Strategic Problem Solvers represent only about 10% of the population, making them one of the rarest personality types.

Your child's personality type:

Adventurous Free Spirit
Seize the day!

Adventurous Free Spirits love to have fun and tend to not take things too seriously. Rather than make plans in advance, they prefer to be spontaneous and respond to whatever is happening in the moment. As a result, they can be impulsive and take more risks than their parents are comfortable with. Adventurous Free Spirit children learn best by doing, rather than by reading or listening to a lecture. The more physical and tactile the experience, the more lasting impression it will leave on this type of child.

Many Adventurous Free Spirits are naturally competitive, like to win, and tend to not be especially concerned about how the person they defeat may feel about their loss. Most of these kids are quite physical, enjoying sports and being in nature. They also may like to take things apart to see how they work—and can usually figure out how to put them back together again. These are kids who don't like being told what to do and are likely to bend the rules whenever they think they can get away with it. These children can also be impulsive and do things that seemed like a good idea…at the time.

Adventurous Free Spirits represent about 18% of the population.

How you're similar to and different from your child

In general, the more similar two people's personality types, the easier, though not necessarily better, the relationship. Three similarities and differences have the greatest impact: how people perceive the world, their core motivators, and their preferred communication style.

It's probably no surprise to you that you and your child are quite different from one another; you are hard-wired to see the world in very different ways. Adventurous Free Spirits observe the world primarily through their five senses. They focus on what is happening in the moment, not what might be in the future. For example, your high-school-senior son decides to take an easier course so he can play sports, not factoring in how this might affect his chances of getting into his first-choice college next year.

Strategic Problem Solvers' minds operate very differently. They rely heavily on their sixth sense to take in information, focusing less on what is than why it is and how it is connected to other things. The difference in how these two types perceive can often lead to huge misunderstandings and explain why you and your child don't always appreciate the other's point of view.

Another important difference is in your varied motivators, which often determine the behaviors and activities that give you the greatest satisfaction. The key motivator for most Strategic Problem Solvers is being successful, which they achieve by being lifelong learners and constantly challenging themselves. Adventurous Free Spirits, on the other hand, derive their greatest satisfaction from having fun and living in the moment. As an example, you may encourage your daughter to follow in your footsteps and become a lawyer so she'll have a secure financial future, but what she really loves is anything that has to do with sports. She realizes that her playing days won't last forever but thinks it would really be fun to coach high school volleyball, even though she won't make as much money.

One of the most significant differences between you and your child are your temperaments, the innate qualities that influence a person's values and key motivators. Adjectives often used to describe the Strategic Problem Solver's temperament are competent, confident, intellectual, independent, high-achieving, strategic, and competitive. Adventurous Free Spirits are most often described as fun-loving, risk-taking, spontaneous, active, adaptable, and impulsive.

Another component is the very different ways your two types communicate and prefer to be communicated with. Adventurous Free Spirits tend to talk about real things they are experiencing in the present, and their speech is usually straightforward and concise. Since Strategic Problem Solvers like big ideas and often string several thoughts together in one sentence, it's not surprising that their Adventurous Free Spirit child may find them unclear and confusing. On the other hand, Strategic Problem Solver parents may be frustrated when their child gets so mired in the details that they fail to understand the larger issue being discussed.

How this may play out in your relationship

All parents want what's best for their kids. Often, mostly unconsciously, parents believe their children will be happier and more successful by being more like them. But what happens when your child is very different from you?

Many child psychologists believe that the happiest, healthiest children are those whose parents really understand and appreciate them for the unique individuals they are. This is what fosters self-esteem. Of course, the opposite is also true: when children are not seen for who they are or appreciated and celebrated for their gifts, they often grow up not feeling good about themselves—or not good enough, in general.

Because Strategic Problem Solvers tend to be over-achievers, they usually set very high standards for themselves and others, especially their children. But your Adventurous Free Spirit child is simply not hard-wired like you and probably lacks your natural gifts of creativity, analytical thinking, and ambition, although they are equipped with their own, different gifts. For these kids, your standards are often difficult and may be impossible to reach, despite how hard they try. For example, getting good grades is often a priority for Strategic Problem Solver parents but seldom matters as much to their Adventurous Free Spirit child.

Compounding this dynamic and setting parent and child up for conflict is that Adventurous Free Spirit children learn very differently from the ways in which traditional schools teach. Most of these kids have strong kinesthetic intelligence, which means they're often good at physical activities like sports, dance, and crafts, and they learn best by doing and experiencing things, rather than by reading or listening to someone talk. A rather common scenario is that Strategic Problem Solver parents want their child to get a college education, but the Adventurous Free Spirit child would prefer a job requiring less or different education because they'd get greater satisfaction from working with their hands or bodies, preferably in an environment where they'll have a lot of autonomy to do the job their way.

Potential vulnerabilities

Research shows that Adventurous Free Spirits may be at slightly higher-than-average risk for anxiety and depression and may also be more affected by online bullying. But not all Adventurous Free Spirits are created equal, and some may be at even greater risk than others. However, because every individual is unique, your child may not necessarily be at increased or decreased risk.

How to nurture your child

"Meet your child where they are." Great advice: easy to give, and much harder to do! Stretching outside of one's comfort zone is hard and may take some practice, especially when the parent's and child's personality types are very different. But it is no less important than making sure your child is safe, clothed, or fed and may be more critical to protecting their mental health and promoting their wellbeing.

We all have gifts that make us special and for which we desperately want to be appreciated. As a Strategic Problem Solver, you're probably proud of your intelligence, creativity, and ability to easily see how things can be improved. But your Adventurous Free Spirit child's greatest gifts are likely very different. They are keen observers of what's happening around them, quick to act, and often very good in a crisis. Recognizing and appreciating your child's greatest gifts lets them know that you see and love them for who they are.

Adventurous Free Spirit children are often not very in tune with their feelings and may feel uncomfortable sharing them. In this respect, you and your child may be quite similar. Conversations involving emotions and the sharing of feelings may be equally uncomfortable for both of you. However, all children need a trusted adult to help them make sense of situations they don't understand, especially things that frighten them.

Many Strategic Problem Solver parents find having such conversations out of their comfort zone. If this is true for you, try to frame this as a challenge to embrace, because it can have such a huge impact on your child's mental health and wellbeing and bring the two of you closer together.

You may find that another parent or trusted adult is more naturally equipped to have these conversations. In instances like this, the Strategic Problem Solver parent may learn a lot and sharpen their skills by watching and listening to how the other person talks to your child.

When trying to engage your Adventurous Free Spirit child in a conversation, they are more likely to respond to specific questions rooted in reality, rather than hypothetical ones that require them to use their imagination. For example, if you ask them "What do you think Jason will do if you tell him he hurt your feelings?" you're likely to be met with a blank stare, followed by "I don't know." (Because they don't.) But if you ask them "Have you told Jason that he hurt your feelings?" followed by "What did he say (or do)?" you'll have a better chance of getting them to provide additional information that will help you have a more productive conversation.

With that said, here are:

Tried and true suggestions for engaging your Adventurous Free Spirit.

- Use fun activities and treats to reward positive behavior; turn chores into games and make them fun whenever possible.
- Recognize that they learn best by experiencing things firsthand.
- Teach them how to take reasonable risks, steering them toward activities that excite, but aren't like to injure, them.
- Don't misinterpret a lack of overt affection as a lack of love and caring.
- Set crystal-clear boundaries, and show them what you mean, rather than simply telling them.

This information is provided for educational purposes only and is not meant to diagnose any condition, or explain or predict any future behavior or conditions in children or adults of any personality type, as each person is a unique individual.

CHAPTER 13
Strategic Problem Solver Parent (Type 2) & Gentle Humble Helper Child (Type 4)

Of course, you know your child better than anyone! But with some types of children, regardless of how diligent the parent is, it's almost impossible to know what's going on beneath the surface. This Parent/Child Profile provides important new insights into your child, yourself, and how your similarities and differences affect your interactions, all with an eye toward helping you build the healthiest, most fulfilling relationship possible.

Your personality type:

Strategic Problem Solver
Everything can be improved.

Strategic Problem Solvers tend to be independent, strong-willed, and competitive. Their love of learning drives them to excel and often results in their being overachievers. Their thought processes can be complex; they connect the dots quite easily and are usually gifted at seeing how things can be improved.

Strategic Problem Solvers may be challenging to interact with because they often like to argue or push back, especially when something doesn't make sense or seem fair to them. Because they're driven to be the best, they set high standards for themselves and others. They usually come across as confident and self-assured, but they may also appear somewhat aloof and often don't show affection easily.

One finds Strategic Problem Solvers in all occupations, but they often gravitate to work that allows them to be independent, continue to learn, solve problems creatively, advance in the organization, and be recognized and well compensated for their competence. A high percentage of them are found in leadership positions. Specific fields that often attract this type include college-level teaching, research, law, technology, economics and finance, science, psychiatry, architecture, and consulting.

Strategic Problem Solvers represent only about 10% of the population, making them one of the rarest personality types.

Your child's personality type:

Gentle Humble Helper
Practice random acts of kindness.

Gentle Humble Helpers tend to be easy-going, warm, kind-hearted, and modest. They are very sensitive and feel things deeply but are likely to share their feelings only with people they trust. These are kids who like to please others and avoid conflict at all costs. They are usually very loyal friends who are good at sharing their toys and possessions.

Gentle Humble Helpers are natural nurturers. They usually get great pleasure from helping others, especially younger children, and are often drawn to and fond of caring for animals. These are fairly realistic kids, and so their play often tends to be more physical, like playing sports, climbing trees, and playing hide-and-seek, rather than engaging in word games or making up imaginary scenarios.

Gentle Humble Helpers usually have a good sense of humor, but if they make jokes, it is seldom at anyone else's expense. They like being spontaneous and responding to what comes up rather than making plans for the future. They can also be impulsive, doing things that seem like a good idea…at the time.

Gentle Humble Helpers represent only about 9% of the population, making them the rarest of the five personality types.

How you're similar to and different from your child

In general, the more similar two people's personality types, the easier, though not necessarily better, the relationship. Three similarities and differences have the greatest impact: how people perceive the world, their core motivators, and their preferred communication style.

It's probably no surprise that you and your child are quite different from one another; you are hard-wired to see the world in very different ways. Gentle Humble Helpers take in information primarily through their five senses. They focus on what is happening right now, not what might be sometime in the future.

Strategic Problem Solvers' minds operate very differently! They rely heavily on their sixth sense to take in information, focusing less on what it is than on why it is and how it is connected to other things. The difference in how these two types perceive can often lead to huge misunderstandings and explains why they don't always appreciate the other's point of view.

Another important difference is in their varied motivators, which often determine the behaviors and activities that give them the greatest satisfaction. The key motivator for most Strategic Problem Solvers is being successful, which they achieve by being lifelong learners and constantly challenging themselves. Gentle Humble Helpers, on the other hand, derive their greatest satisfaction from helping people in real and practical ways. A good example would be that you encourage your daughter to go to law school so she'll have a secure financial future, but she loves working with kids and wants to teach elementary school, even though she won't make as much money.

One of the most significant differences between these two types are their temperaments, the innate qualities that influence their values and key motivators. Adjectives often used to describe the Strategic Problem Solver's temperament are competent, confident, intellectual, independent, strategic, high-achieving, and competitive. Gentle Humble Helpers are most often described as fun-loving, caring, kind, nurturing, spontaneous, and adaptable.

When it comes to communicating, Gentle Humble Helpers tend to be concise and straightforward and like to talk about real things rather than ideas or concepts. But Strategic Problem Solvers' communication style is quite different. They love talking about ideas, and their conversations often include lots of different thoughts linked together. As a result, your Gentle Humble Helper child may find your message unclear and confusing. By contrast, as a Strategic Problem Solver, you may feel that your child sometimes gets so mired in the details that they fail to see the larger issue and what the conversation is really all about.

How this may play out in your relationship

All parents want what's best for their kids. Often, mostly unconsciously, parents believe their children will be happier and more successful by being more like them. But what happens when your child is very different from you?

Many child psychologists believe that the happiest, healthiest children are those whose parents really understand and appreciate them for the unique individuals they are. This is what fosters self-esteem. Of course, the opposite is also true: when children are not seen for who they are or appreciated and celebrated for their gifts, they often grow up not feeling good about themselves—or not good enough, in general.

Because Strategic Problem Solvers tend to be over-achievers, they usually set very high standards for themselves and others, especially their children. But your Gentle Humble Helper child is simply not hard-wired like you, and probably lacks your natural gifts of creativity, analytical thinking, and ambition, though they certainly do have their own, different gifts. It's quite possible that your standards may be impossible for them to reach, no matter how hard they try. For example, getting good grades is likely to be a priority for you as a Strategic Problem Solver but is likely to be less so for your Gentle Humble Helper child.

Compounding this dynamic and setting parent and child up for conflict is that Gentle Humble Helper children learn very differently from the ways in which traditional schools teach. Most of these children have strong kinesthetic intelligence, which means they're often good at physical activities like sports, dance, and crafts, and they learn best by doing and experiencing things, rather than by reading or listening to people talk. A rather common scenario is that Strategic Problem Solver parents want their child to get a college education, but the Gentle Humble Helper child would prefer a job requiring less or different education because they'd get greater satisfaction from working with their hands.

Potential vulnerabilities

Research shows that Gentle Humble Helpers have a higher-than-average risk for anxiety and depression and may also be more affected by online bullying. But not all Gentle Humble Helpers are created equal; some may be at even greater risk than others. However, because every individual is unique, your child may not necessarily be at increased or decreased risk.

How to nurture your child

"Meet your child where they are." Great advice: easy to give, and much harder to do! Stretching outside of one's comfort zone is hard and may take some practice, especially when the parent's and child's personality types are very different. But it is no less important than making sure your child is safe, clothed, or fed and may be more critical to protecting their mental health and promoting their wellbeing.

We all have gifts that make us special and for which we desperately want to be appreciated. As a Strategic Problem Solver, you're probably proud of your intelligence, creativity, and ability to easily see how things can be improved. But your Gentle Humble Helper's greatest gift is likely their ability to be a helpful, loyal friend, which is very different from yours! Recognizing and appreciating your child's greatest gifts lets them know that you see and love them for who they are.

Remember that Gentle Humble Helpers are extremely sensitive but have a hard time sharing their feelings; getting them to open up can be very challenging—but critically important. Due to their hard-wiring, most Strategic Problem Solver parents find having conversations that involve emotions and deep feelings out of their comfort zone. If this is true for you, try to frame this as a challenge to embrace, because it can have such a huge impact on your child's mental health and wellbeing and bring the two of you closer together.

You may find that another parent or trusted adult is naturally equipped to have these conversations. In instances like this, the Strategic Problem Solver parent may learn a lot and sharpen their skills by watching and listening to how the other person talks to your child.

Your Strategic Problem Solver child probably has a rich imagination, which they enjoy using. Asking them to help brainstorm solutions to a problem they share with you (especially if they're more extraverted) is more likely to get them engaged, and you're likely to learn more about what's going on in their life, as well.

With that said, here are:

Tried and true suggestions for engaging your Gentle Humble Helper:

- Smile, give them lots of hugs and kisses, and frequently tell them you love them.
- Give them very specific directions and instructions and show them what you mean whenever possible.
- Accept their need to be physically active. Play with them and surprise them; be spontaneous.

- Support their feelings and allow them to express them in their own time and style.
- Use incentives and rewards that are tangible, such as fun activities, freedom, money, and treats.

This information is provided for educational purposes only and is not meant to diagnose any condition, or explain or predict any future behavior or conditions in children or adults of any personality type, as each person is a unique individual.

CHAPTER 14
Strategic Problem Solver Parent (Type 2) & Creative Sensitive Soul Child (Type 5)

Of course, you know your child better than anyone! But with some types of children, regardless of how diligent the parent is, it's almost impossible to know what's going on beneath the surface. This Parent/Child Profile provides important new insights into your child, yourself, and how your similarities and differences affect your interactions, all with an eye toward helping you build the healthiest, most fulfilling relationship possible.

Your personality type:

Strategic Problem Solver
Everything can be improved.

Strategic Problem Solvers tend to be independent, strong-willed, and competitive. Their love of learning drives them to excel and often results in their being overachievers. Their thought processes can be complex; they connect the dots quite easily and are usually gifted at seeing how things can be improved.

Strategic Problem Solvers may be challenging to interact with because they often like to argue or push back, especially when something doesn't make sense or seem fair to them. Because they're driven to be the best, they set high standards for themselves and others. They usually come across as confident and self-assured, but they may also appear somewhat aloof and often don't show affection easily.

One finds Strategic Problem Solvers in all occupations, but they often gravitate to work that allows them to be independent, continue to learn, solve problems creatively, advance in the organization,

and be recognized and well compensated for their competence. A high percentage of them are found in leadership positions. Specific fields that often attract this type include college-level teaching, research, law, technology, economics and finance, science, psychiatry, architecture, and consulting.

Strategic Problem Solvers represent only about 10% of the population, making them one of the rarest personality types.

Your child's personality type:

Creative Sensitive Soul
Seeing possibilities everywhere.

Creative Sensitive Souls feel things deeply and are very empathetic. As a result, they avoid conflict and try to make people happy, often putting others' needs ahead of their own. Because these children often feel things more intensely than other types of children, they can feel lonely and sometimes sense that they don't quite belong.

Because Creative Sensitive Souls have vivid imaginations and feel things so deeply, they are the most idealistic of all the types. They know the way things should be (but seldom are), which can cause them to become moody, disillusioned, or depressed. Usually loving and physically affectionate, they may also be easily frightened and prone to worrying.

Many Creative Sensitive Souls are, as their name implies, creative, which they may express through art, music, poetry, dance, acting, and other such endeavors. They often have vivid imaginations, and when they're young they may like to play games that begin with "Let's pretend..." They tend to take things personally and can be moody and easily upset when criticized.

Creative Sensitive Souls represent about 17% of the population.

How you're similar to and different from your child

In general, the more similar two people's personality types, the easier, though not necessarily better, the relationship. Three similarities and differences have the greatest impact: how people perceive the world, their core motivators, and their preferred communication style.

It's probably no surprise to you that you and your child are quite different from one another. But in a consequential way, you're similar. Both you and your Creative Sensitive Soul child rely heavily on your intuition or your sixth sense when you're taking in information, focusing less on current realities than on future possibilities. Both of you naturally connect the dots, see the big picture, and understand how things are related to one another. Sharing the way you see the world means you usually understand each other, though you may not necessarily like or agree with what the other is saying.

But your primary motivation, which can influence your values, can also be quite different. For most Strategic Problem Solvers, the key motivator is being successful, which they achieve by being lifelong learners and constantly challenging themselves. Creative Sensitive Soul, on the other hand, derive their greatest satisfaction from being authentic and empathetic and finding meaning and purpose in what they do. For example, you encourage your daughter to go to law school so she'll have a secure financial future, but she feels called to teach disadvantaged children who have not had the same opportunities she's had and can benefit from her gifts.

Your types also have different temperaments, often considered the core of one's personality type, which influence your values, competencies, and interests. Some words that are often used to describe the temperament of Strategic Problem Solvers include competent, confident, independent, intellectual, high achieving, and strategic. Adjectives most often used to describe Creative Sensitive Souls are empathetic, idealistic, perceptive, creative, spiritual, compassionate, and collaborative.

Another difference is how the two of you communicate and prefer to be communicated with. Being as empathetic as they are, Creative Sensitive Souls are very perceptive about how others are feeling and driven to try to make them feel better. They are also much more likely to take even mild and constructive criticism personally.

In contrast, being good at objectively analyzing a situation and quickly seeing solutions, Strategic Problem Solvers may not pay much attention to how others are feeling, and they may not be comfortable providing emotional support. They usually have much thicker skin and are not often affected if they're criticized.

How this may play out in your relationship

All parents want what's best for their kids. Often, mostly unconsciously, parents believe their children will be happier and more successful by being more like them. But what happens when your child is very different from you?

Many child psychologists believe that the happiest, healthiest children are those whose parents really understand and appreciate them for the unique individuals they are. This is what fosters self-esteem. Of course, the opposite is also true: when children are not seen for who they are or appreciated and celebrated for their gifts, they often grow up not feeling good about themselves—or not good enough, in general.

Strategic Problem Solvers tend to be high (some might say over) achievers, usually setting very high standards for themselves and others, especially their children. But Creative Sensitive Souls can also be high achievers, although the parent may not recognize or appreciate that fact if their child's interests don't align with their own desires or expectations. For example, Strategic Problem Solvers typically place a high value on academic success. But if a Creative Sensitive Soul child doesn't feel the same way, the parent may inadvertently send them the message that they're not good enough, perhaps that they lack ambition or self-discipline. Such messages can have serious consequences and lead some children to spend their whole lives trying to gain their parent's approval.

For the logical Strategic Problem Solvers, feelings are valid—if they make sense. For example, if a child gets bullied, the parent can understand why he is sad. But if the child is upset because they didn't get invited to the birthday party of a classmate they don't really like all that much, that same parent may not understand why their child still feels rejected and may try to talk the child out of their feelings.

Along the same lines, Strategic Problem Solvers, as the name implies, are gifted at coming up with good solutions, often very quickly. But often the Creative Sensitive Soul child may just need to vent how they're feeling and not have their parent immediately try to fix the problem.

Potential vulnerabilities

Research shows that Creative Sensitive Souls may be at significantly higher risk for anxiety and depression and may also be more affected by bullying, both in person and online. But not all Creative Sensitive Souls are created equal, and some may be at greater risk than others. However, because every individual is unique, your child may not necessarily be at increased or decreased risk.

How to nurture your child

"Meet your child where they are." Great advice: easy to give, and much harder to do! Stretching outside of one's comfort zone is hard and may take some practice, especially when the parent's and child's personality types are very different. But it is no less important than making sure your child is safe, clothed, or fed and may be more critical to protecting their mental health and promoting their wellbeing.

We all have gifts that make us special and for which we desperately want to be appreciated. As a Strategic Problem Solver, you're probably proud of your intelligence, creativity, and ability to easily see how things can be improved. But your Creative Sensitive Souls greatest gift is likely their empathy and being true to themselves and their beliefs. Recognizing and appreciating your child's greatest gifts lets them know that you see and love them for who they are.

It's very important for Strategic Problem Solver parents to remember that their Creative Sensitive Soul child is extremely sensitive but may have a hard time sharing their feelings. Perhaps you've heard the expression "still waters run deep." There is always a lot going on inside these children. More extraverted Creative Sensitive Soul children are usually more likely to share and hence may be easier to read. But if your child is more introverted, it can be very challenging to understand the depth of their feelings, but critically important that you do so.

A special word to Strategic Problem Solver parents: you may find having emotional conversations difficult and outside your comfort zone. But try to frame doing this as a challenge to embrace, because it can have such a huge impact on your child's mental health and wellbeing and also bring the two of you closer together.

In many families, one parent might naturally be better at dealing with emotions. If this is the case, the other parent can learn to communicate more effectively by watching and listening to how that parent interacts with their child.

Both you and your Creative Sensitive Soul child probably have a rich imagination, which you enjoy using. Asking your child to help brainstorm solutions to a problem they share with you (especially if they're more extraverted) is more likely to get them engaged, and you're likely to learn more about what's going on in their life, as well.

With that said, here are:

Tried and true suggestions for engaging your Creative Sensitive Soul:

- Try not to judge or rush them through their feelings.
- Appreciate their individuality and express your love and affection frequently.
- Forgive them quickly and never give them the silent treatment.
- Encourage them to speak their truth and not feel they have to have to sugarcoat things.
- Listen to and support their ideas; don't squelch their creativity or originality.

This information is provided for educational purposes only and is not meant to diagnose any condition, or explain or predict any future behavior or conditions in children or adults of any personality type, as each person is a unique individual.

Adventurous Free Spirit Parent

and their Child Personality Types

CHAPTER 15
Adventurous Free Spirit Parent (Type 3) & Responsible Hard Worker Child (Type 1)

Of course, you know your child better than anyone! But with some types of children, regardless of how diligent the parent, it's almost impossible to know what's going on beneath the surface. This Parent/Child Profile provides important new insights into your child, yourself, and how your similarities and differences affect your interactions, all with an eye toward helping you build the healthiest, most fulfilling relationship possible.

Your personality type:

Adventurous Free Spirit
Seize the Day!

Adventurous Free Spirits love to have fun and tend to not take things too seriously or sweat the small stuff. Rather than make plans too far in advance, they like to be free to be spontaneous and respond to whatever is happening in the moment. As a result, they can be impulsive and take more risks than others may be comfortable with.

Adventurous Free Spirits tend to be competitive and like winning, and they are usually not especially concerned about how those they defeat may feel about their loss. Many are quite physical, enjoying sports and being in nature. They also may like to take things apart to see how they work—and are usually able to put them back together. They cherish their freedom and don't like being micromanaged or told what to do; nor do they have difficulty bending the rules when that seems to them like a reasonable thing to do.

One finds Adventurous Free Spirits in all occupations, but they

often gravitate to work that affords them a lot of freedom and excitement, that includes physical activity, a variety of tasks, and the opportunity to use specific skills they've mastered, and that doesn't require excessive supervision. Some fields that often attract people of this type include being a first responder (police officer, firefighter, EMT), athletic coach, sports commentator, builder, trial attorney, tradesperson, surgeon, or stock trader.

Adventurous Free Spirits represent about 18% of the population.

Your child's personality type:

Responsible Hard Worker
Always do the right thing

Responsible Hard Workers tend to be serious and cautious. They like familiar routines and traditions. By their nature, they like structure and boundaries and tend to follow the rules, and they expect others to follow them, too.

As children and adolescents, Responsible Hard Workers are usually not especially challenging to parent. They tend to be fairly compliant when it comes to doing their chores, finishing their homework, and helping out with younger siblings. They usually take their responsibilities, such as caring for their pets, seriously.

Responsible Hard Workers usually respect authority figures such as parents, teachers, doctors, and police officers, and they don't tend to push the envelope or rock the boat. They have a strong sense of duty and often feel an obligation to help others. They're most comfortable when plans have been made and can get upset when plans are changed, especially at the last minute. They are usually driven to finish whatever they start, such as games, art projects, or puzzles.

Responsible Hard Workers represent about 46% of the population, making them the most common personality type.

How you're similar to and different from your child

In general, the more similar two people's personality types, the easier, though not necessarily better, the relationship. Three similarities and differences have the greatest impact: how people perceive the world, their core motivators, and their preferred communication style.

You probably find that you and your child are very different types of people.

Both **Adventurous Free Spirit** parents and their **Responsible Hard Worker** children take in information primarily through their five senses, which tends to make them realistic and practical. They focus on what is happening in the moment, not what might be in the future. For example, it's likely that you both may share interests that involve being physical, like sports, hiking, biking, or working on cars, rather than writing poetry together or having deep philosophical discussions.

An important difference is in what motivates the two of you, which often influences the behaviors and activities that give you your greatest satisfaction. Most **Adventurous Free Spirits** like you derive their greatest satisfaction from being free to simply be present and enjoy their lives with as little supervision as possible. They love to be able to respond spontaneously when a fun activity presents itself. **Responsible Hard Workers,** on the other hand, derive great satisfaction from taking on a specific task and accomplishing it. As an example, while you might have put off cleaning out the garage for months, your **Responsible Hard Worker** child may actually enjoy taking on the task, especially if they're complimented—and compensated for—doing a good job.

One of the most significant differences between these two types is their temperament–innate qualities that influence a person's values and key motivators. Words that are most often used to describe **Adventurous Free Spirits** are fun-loving, risk-taking, spontaneous, active, adaptable, and impulsive. In contrast, adjectives often used to describe your **Responsible Hard Worker** child's temperament are dependable, organized, productive, service-oriented, trustworthy, traditional, and consistent.

Another component describes the different ways your two types communicate and prefer to be communicated with. In many ways, your communication styles are quite similar.

Both **Adventurous Free Spirits** and **Responsible Hard Workers** tend to communicate in a direct, straightforward manner, preferring to talk about practical realities rather than abstract ideas. Although they may not always agree, they seldom have a hard time understanding what the other is saying. Although their styles are similar, what they choose to talk about can be quite different. Because **Adventurous Free Spirits** tend to be logical and analytical, they may focus on more impersonal things and situations. But if your Responsible Hard Worker child is more sensitive, they may want to talk more about a recent experience they had with classmates, friends, or family members.

How this may play out in your relationship

All parents want what's best for their kids. Often, mostly unconsciously, parents believe their children will be happier and more successful by being more like them. But what happens when your child is very different from you?

Many child psychologists believe that the happiest, healthiest children are those whose parents really understand and appreciate them for the unique individuals they are. This is what fosters self-esteem. Of course, the opposite is also true: when children are not seen for who they are or appreciated and celebrated for their gifts, they often grow up not feeling good about themselves—or not good enough, in general.

Both Adventurous Free Spirit parents and their Responsible Hard Worker children have what is known as kinesthetic intelligence: they're usually good at using their bodies to express themselves, to learn, and to solve problems. They're often adept at physical activities and learn best through hands-on experiences, which is the main reason they are often drawn to sports or enjoy being in nature.

Although similar in many ways, there are some notable differences between Adventurous Free Spirits and Responsible Hard Workers. You probably prefer to be more spontaneous, while your child feels more comfortable having, and following, a plan and can get quite upset when plans are not followed or are changed at the last minute, especially without their being notified. For example, you may tell your daughter you'll pick her up from soccer practice at 5:00 but are running late, which may happen frequently with Adventurous Free Spirits, and don't show up until 5:20. Although you may consider this no big deal, it may be quite upsetting to her.

Most Responsible Hard Worker children love traditions and rituals because they are predictable and make them feel safe. Responsible Hard Worker children tend to be much more cautious than their more impulsive, risk-taking Adventurous Free Spirit parents. Without being aware of this, you run the risk of shaming your child if they don't feel comfortable or safe trying some activity you encourage them to do. As an example, you may urge your daughter to try out your neighbor's new zip line, which you'd love to do but is something that scares her.

Another area of potential conflict may revolve around your different views concerning work and play. Adventurous Free Spirit parents often love to be able to respond to some new opportunity, even if that might mean interrupting a chore they're working on. But Responsible Hard Workers have a strong need to finish what they start, even if that means missing out on something that might be more fun. This is a fundamental difference between parents and children of these two types, so it's important for parents to understand and respect that their child's priorities may be different from their own.

Potential vulnerabilities

Although every individual is unique, research shows that most Responsible Hard Workers have a lower-than-average risk of developing anxiety and depression and may be less susceptible to others' negative online behavior. But it's important to note there are two varieties of Responsible Hard Workers: Thinkers tend to make most of their decisions based on logic, whereas Feelers base most of their decisions on how they feel about something and how they and others will be affected. Responsible Hard Workers who are Feelers may be more susceptible to anxiety, depression, and bullying than those who are Thinkers. But every individual is unique. Therefore, this does not mean that your child is necessarily at increased or decreased risk.

How to nurture your child

"Meet your child where they are." Great advice: easy to give, and much harder to do! Stretching outside of one's comfort zone is hard and may take some practice, especially when the parent's and child's personality types are very different. But it is no less important than making sure your child is safe, clothed, or fed and may be more critical to protecting their mental health and promoting their wellbeing.

We all have gifts that make us special and for which we want to be appreciated—and celebrated. As an Adventurous Free Spirit, among your greatest gifts are your ability to be in the moment, keenly observe what's going on around you, enjoy whatever you're doing, and help others too as well. You'll probably take it as a compliment if someone were to say, "You are so much fun! I always have a good time when I'm with you!"

But your Responsible Hard Worker's greatest gifts are their

strong work ethic and that they can be counted on to do whatever they say they will, when they say they'll do it. Recognizing and appreciating your child's greatest gifts lets them know that you see and love them for who they are. Responsible Hard Workers would consider it a greater compliment if someone were to tell them, "You did such a great job with that project! Clearly you worked hard, and it shows!"

As mentioned above, there are two varieties of Responsible Hard Workers: Thinkers and Feelers. You may find it a little easier to communicate with your Responsible Hard Worker if they are a Thinker like you, because you both tend not to take things personally and have pretty thick skins. But if your Responsible Hard Worker is a Feeler, you will need to stretch beyond your comfort zone, tune in to how they are feeling, and approach them more sensitively.

If one parent is a Feeler, they may be better at gently coaxing your child to open up to them. If this is the case, then the other parent may be able to learn to communicate more effectively by watching and listening to how that parent interacts with their child.

When trying to engage your Responsible Hard Worker child in a conversation, know that they are more likely to respond to specific questions, rooted in reality, rather than hypothetical ones that require them to use their imagination. For example, if you ask them "What do you think Jason will do if you tell him he hurt your feelings?" you're likely to be met with a blank stare, followed by "I don't know." (Because they don't.) But if you ask them "Have you told Jason that he hurt your feelings?" followed by "What did he say (or do)?" you'll have a better chance of getting them to provide additional information that will help you have a more productive conversation.

With that said, here are:

Tried and true suggestions for engaging your Responsible Hard Worker:

- Be clear and explicit in your directions and requests; say what you mean and mean what you say.
- Prepare them in advance for new experiences and changes in plans.
- Recognize you both want to be, and often are, right. Learn to back off and to choose your battles.

- Be on time; follow through on all your commitments to them.
- Encourage them to question things rather than always taking things at face value.
- Reward them with increasing levels of responsibility and praise them for their accomplishments.

This information is provided for educational purposes only and is not meant to diagnose any condition, or explain or predict any future behavior or conditions in children or adults of any personality type, as each person is a unique individual.

CHAPTER 16
Adventurous Free Spirit Parent (Type 3) & Strategic Problem Solver Child (Type 2)

Of course, you know your child better than anyone! But with some types of children, regardless of how diligent the parent, it's almost impossible to know what's going on beneath the surface. This Parent/Child Profile provides important new insights into your child, yourself, and how your similarities and differences affect your interactions, all with an eye toward helping you build the healthiest, most fulfilling relationship possible.

Your personality type:

Adventurous Free Spirit
Seize the Day!

Adventurous Free Spirits love to have fun and tend to not take things too seriously or sweat the small stuff. Rather than make plans too far in advance, they like to be free to be spontaneous and respond to whatever is happening in the moment. As a result, they can be impulsive and take more risks than others may be comfortable with.

Adventurous Free Spirits tend to be competitive and like winning, and they are usually not especially concerned about how those they defeat may feel about their loss. Many are quite physical, enjoying sports and being in nature. They also may like to take things apart to see how they work—and are usually able to put them back together. They cherish their freedom and don't like being micromanaged or told what to do; nor do they have difficulty bending the rules when that seems to them like a reasonable thing to do.

One finds Adventurous Free Spirits in all occupations, but they

often gravitate to work that affords them a lot of freedom and excitement, that includes physical activity, a variety of tasks, and the opportunity to use specific skills they've mastered, and that doesn't require excessive supervision. Some fields that often attract people of this type include being a first responder (police officer, firefighter, EMT), athletic coach, sports commentator, builder, trial attorney, tradesperson, surgeon, or stock trader.

Adventurous Free Spirits represent about 18% of the population.

Your child's personality type:

Strategic Problem Solver
Everything can be improved.

Strategic Problem Solvers tend to be independent, strong-willed, and competitive. Their thirst for knowledge and love of learning drives them to excel and often results in their being high achievers. Their thought process can be complex, and they connect most dots quite easily. As a result, they love to figure things out and find ways to improve upon them, and they are usually gifted at doing so.

Strategic Problem Solvers can be challenging to parent because they often like to argue or push back, especially when something doesn't make sense or seems unfair to them. Because they're driven to be the best, they're usually good at whatever interests them, but they can become bored if they're not adequately challenged. They usually come across as confident and self-assured but may also appear somewhat aloof, and they often don't show affection easily. Logical and analytical, Strategic Problem Solvers are often very objective and don't tend to take things personally.

Strategic Problem Solvers represent only about 10% of the population, making them one of the rarest personality types.

How you're similar to and different from your child

In general, the more similar two people's personality types, the easier, though not necessarily better, the relationship. Three similarities and differences have the greatest impact: how people perceive the world, their core motivators, and their preferred communication style.

It's probably no surprise that you and your child are quite different. Adventurous Free Spirits take in information primarily through their five senses. They focus on what is happening in the moment, not what might occur sometime in the future. But Strategic Problem Solvers rely heavily on their intuition or sixth sense to take in information, focusing less on what is than what is possible, what something means and how it is connected to other things. For example, your son may constantly surprise you with how many topics he seems to know so much about and appear to be an expert in, until he finds something else fascinating to learn about. His insatiable curiosity and ability to learn new, often complicated things quickly may become his superpower! The more he is praised for this quality, the better he will feel about himself—and you.

Another important difference is in what motivates the two of you, which often influences the behaviors and activities that give you your greatest satisfaction.

Most Adventurous Free Spirits derive their greatest satisfaction from being free to simply be present and enjoy their lives with as few rules and people telling them what to do as possible, whereas most Strategic Problem Solvers derive their greatest satisfaction from continuing to learn new things, developing new competencies, and being successful. They are especially engaged when, faced with a challenge, they can come up with an innovative solution.

One of the most significant differences between you and your child are your temperaments, innate qualities that influence a person's values and key motivators. Adjectives often used to describe Adventurous Free Spirits such as you are fun-loving, risk-taking, spontaneous, active, adaptable, responsive, and impulsive. In contrast, words most often used to describe your Strategic Problem Solver child are competent, confident, intellectual, independent, high-achieving, strategic, and competitive.

Another component is the different ways your two types communicate and prefer to be communicated with.

Adventurous Free Spirits are typically not gifted communicators, for a couple of reasons. They are not naturally introspective or reflective, and they think more concretely than abstractly. They tend to focus on what is happening in the moment, not necessarily on its meaning. And they make decisions more objectively than personally. In contrast, Strategic Problem Solvers usually enjoy discussing big, new ideas and possibilities that may occur in the future. Their language tends to be complex, often involving multiple ideas in the same sentence. As a result of these very different styles,

Adventurous Free Spirits often find Strategic Problem Solvers unclear, complicated, and confusing, while Strategic Problem Solvers may find their counterparts get so mired in the details they can fail to see the big picture, nuances, or implications.

How this may play out in your relationship

All parents want what's best for their kids. Often, mostly unconsciously, parents believe their children will be happier and more successful by being more like them. But what happens when your child is very different from you?

Many child psychologists believe that the happiest, healthiest children are those whose parents really understand and appreciate them for the unique individuals they are. This is what fosters self-esteem. Of course, the opposite is also true: when children are not seen for who they are or appreciated and celebrated for their gifts, they often grow up not feeling good about themselves—or not good enough, in general.

Many Adventurous Free Spirit parents have what is known as kinesthetic intelligence. This means that they excel at using their bodies to express themselves, learn, and solve problems. They're often adept at physical activities and learn best through hands-on experiences. As a result, many are drawn to sports and enjoy being in nature. Strategic Problem Solvers are more likely to possess logical-mathematical intelligence, the ability to think logically, analyze problems, perform mathematical operations, recognize patterns, and solve problems using abstract concepts. For example, an Adventurous Free Spirit parent wants to take the family on a camping trip, where his Strategic Problem Solver child might rather attend a science fair.

Strategic Problem Solvers come in two varieties: one, called Judgers, is more focused on plans and likes things decided, while the other, Perceivers, prefer to live more spontaneously and keep their options open. Tensions can arise when Strategic Problem Solvers who are Judgers may feel pressured by their Adventurous Free Spirit parent to lighten up and drop what they're doing to go on some unplanned adventure. As an example, a Strategic Problem Solver daughter is trying to finish an important homework assignment when her Adventurous Free Spirit parent suggests she stop what she's doing and have a snowball fight in the season's first snowfall.

Typically, Adventurous Free Spirits learn by doing, while

Strategic Problem Solvers often learn by reading, studying, and thinking, sometimes quite deeply, about an issue. Most Adventurous Free Spirit parents are simply not hard-wired in the same way, and may lack the interest and patience to have the kind of long, complicated conversations their child enjoys.

The days are long gone when people believed that children should be seen and not heard. However, parents of Strategic Problem Solver children quickly learn that their child is usually not shy about pushing back and expressing their, sometimes very strong, opinions. Although it might not seem like it at the time, they are not doing this to be disrespectful or disruptive. This is simply the way they learn: by questioning, debating, and weighing the pros and cons of any issue or topic.

Potential vulnerabilities

Research shows that Strategic Problem Solvers may have a lower-than-average risk of developing anxiety and depression and may be less susceptible to bullying and other negative online behavior by others. But every individual is unique. Therefore, this does not mean that your child is necessarily at increased or decreased risk.

How to nurture your child

"Meet your child where they are." Great advice: easy to give, and much harder to do! Stretching outside of one's comfort zone is hard and may take some practice, especially when the parent's and child's personality types are very different. But it is no less important than making sure your child is safe, clothed, or fed and may be more critical to protecting their mental health and promoting their wellbeing.

We all have gifts that make us special and for which we want to be appreciated and celebrated. As an Adventurous Free Spirit, among your greatest gifts are your ability to be in the moment, keenly observe what's going on around you, enjoy whatever you're doing, and help others to as well. Among your Strategic Problem Solver child's gifts are usually a quick and agile mind, intellectual curiosity, and the ability to be logical and objective and to quickly grasp complex ideas and concepts. Recognizing and appreciating these gifts lets your child know that you see and love them for who they are, especially if they are very different from you.

Because both you and your child are Thinkers who tend to make decisions based more on logic than feelings or emotions, neither one of you might be especially aware of how you or the other is feeling in the moment. But this doesn't mean that it's not important to try to figure it out and be willing to have conversations you may find uncomfortable. For Strategic Problem Solver children, learning how to get in touch with their feelings is a critical life skill, and it's your job as the parent to help them learn. In some cases, your spouse or partner may be more comfortable having conversations that involve emotions and havean easier time getting the child to open up. If this is true in your family, you may learn an important new skill by observing your more naturally equipped partner.

Your Strategic Problem Solver child probably has a rich imagination that they enjoy using. So asking them to help brainstorm solutions to a problem they share with you (especially if they're more extraverted) is more likely to get them engaged, and you're likely to learn more about what's going on in their life, as well.

With that said, here are:

Tried and true suggestions for engaging your Strategic Problem Solver:

- Compliment them on their creative ideas and logical arguments and be willing to let them win.
- Model open and honest communication of feelings; help them develop kindness, generosity, and tact.
- Expect to be challenged, and respect their strong need for independence.
- Be fair and consistent in discipline; explain the logical, rational reasons for decisions and rules.
- Try not to take a lack of overt affection on their part personally and find common interests to foster closeness and intimacy.
- Reward them with increasing levels of responsibility and praise them for their accomplishments.

This information is provided for educational purposes only and is not meant to diagnose any condition, or explain or predict any future behavior or conditions in children or adults of any personality type, as each person is a unique individual.

CHAPTER 17
Adventurous Free Spirit Parent & Child (Type 3)

Of course, you know your child better than anyone! But with some types of children, regardless of how diligent the parent is, it's almost impossible to know what's going on beneath the surface. This Parent/Child Profile provides important new insights into your child, yourself, and how your similarities and differences affect your interactions, all with an eye toward helping you build the healthiest, most fulfilling relationship possible.

It's relatively rare for children and parents to share the same personality type, but when they do, the two are usually similar in many ways. Personality is a combination of nature—your inborn personality type—and nurture—everything else you experience in life, the greatest influence being your parents. While you and your child may be kindred spirits in many ways, there will be profound differences between the two of you because every person is a unique individual and because of your different ages, generations, experiences, and, most importantly, who you were parented by.

Here is a snapshot of the personality type you share with your child. If after reading this report you think that you may have misidentified your own or your child's type, you may want to revisit Chapter 4.

Your and your child's personality type:

Adventurous Free Spirit
Seize the Day!

Adventurous Free Spirits love to have fun and tend to not take most things too seriously or sweat the small stuff. Rather than make plans too far in advance, they like to be free to be spontaneous and respond to whatever is happening in the moment. As a result, they can be impulsive and take more risks than others may be comfortable with.

Many Adventurous Free Spirits are naturally competitive, like to win, and are usually not terribly concerned about how the person they defeat feels about their loss. Many are quite physical, enjoying sports and being in nature. They also may like to take things apart to see how they work and are usually able to figure out how to put them back together. They cherish their freedom and don't like being micromanaged or told what to do; nor do they have difficulty bending the rules when that seems like a reasonable thing to do.

One finds Adventurous Free Spirits in all occupations, but they often gravitate to work that affords them a lot of freedom and excitement and includes physical activity, a variety of tasks and the opportunity to use specific skills they've mastered, and that does not require excessive supervision. Specific fields that often attract many people of this type include being a first responder (police officer, firefighter, EMT), athletic coach, trial attorney, sports commentator, builder, tradesperson, surgeon, and stock trader.

Adventurous Free Spirits represent about 18% of the population.

Similarities with your child
In general, the more similar two people's personality types, the easier, though not necessarily better, the relationship. Three similarities and differences have the greatest impact: how people perceive the world, their core motivators, and their preferred communication style.

The first commonality is how the two of you prefer to take in information. Adventurous Free Spirits do this primarily through their five senses, focusing on details and specifics. They tend to take most things at face value, which usually makes them realistic, practical, and down to earth. For them, the world is not a terribly complicated place. They pay attention to what's happening in the moment rather than what they imagine might happen sometime in the future.

Most Adventurous Free Spirits derive their greatest satisfaction from being free to simply be present and enjoy their lives with as few rules and people telling them what to do as possible. They love to be able to respond spontaneously when a fun activity presents itself.

Adventurous Free Spirits tend to communicate in a direct, straightforward manner, preferring to talk about practical realities rather than abstract ideas, and because they are quite logical and analytical by nature, they usually provide honest, if occasionally blunt and sometimes undiplomatic, feedback. For example, to be helpful, you may tell your son who just struck out that his batting stance is all wrong. But what he hears is that he's not good enough and has disappointed you.

When it comes to communication, **Adventurous Free Spirits** tend to be concise and straightforward and prefer to talk about real things and events, which almost always focus on people rather than on ideas or concepts, which is another important thing you share. So, while you may not always agree, you'll probably have no trouble understanding where your child is coming from.

When two people of the same type do experience conflict, it's often because they are too similar, having parallel weaknesses and blind spots. Weaknesses are things we know we're not good at, while blind spots are things we are unaware of that cause us to not be as effective as we'd like to be.

You may have noticed that it's not unusual to notice a personal quality or behavior in someone else that annoys you. Often, the reason is that we share that same quality but may not be aware of or able to own it. This can be even more prevalent when two people share the same personality type. It can feel like we're looking in the mirror—and don't necessarily like what we see.

How this may play out in your relationship

All parents want what's best for their children. And often, mostly unconsciously, parents believe their children will be happier and more successful by being more like them.

Many child psychologists believe that the happiest, healthiest children are those whose parents really understand and appreciate them for the unique individuals they are. This is what fosters self-esteem. Of course, the opposite is also true: when children are not seen for who they are or appreciated and celebrated for their gifts, they often grow up not feeling good about themselves—or not good enough, in general.

It's important for parents who share the same type with their child to remember, they may think like you…they may sound like you…they may even look like you…but they are not you. It's easy for some parents to think of their child as a "mini-me," which can cause conflict. Having brains that are similarly hard-wired means you probably will see eye-to-eye on most things but may not have shared interests.

It's helpful to be aware that Adventurous Free Spirits usually prefer to learn by doing, rather than reading and studying, and that your child may be either more or less ambitious academically, or career-wise, than you. This is when it's important to remember that they are not you and need to be supported for their choices.

Potential vulnerabilities

Research shows that Adventurous Free Spirits may have a slightly higher-than-average risk of developing anxiety and depression and be more susceptible to bullying and others' negative online behavior. But because every individual is unique, this does not mean that your child is necessarily at increased or decreased risk.

How to nurture your child

"Meet your child where they are." Great advice: easy to give, and much harder to do! Stretching outside of one's comfort zone is hard and may take some practice, especially when the parent's and child's personality types are very different. But it is no less important than making sure your child is safe, clothed, or fed and may be more critical to protecting their mental health and promoting their wellbeing.

We all have gifts that make us special and for which we want and need to be appreciated. Adventurous Free Spirits are often described as having a joie de vivre – a joy of living. Not only do they enjoy the moment, but they help others too as well. They are also often very helpful in real and practical ways, such as assisting with physical chores or fixing things.

Adventurous Free Spirits can also be adrenalin junkies and like to engage in high-risk activities that give them a rush. "The unexamined life is not worth living" is a quote attributed to Socrates. But Adventurous Free Spirits may relate better to the statement "The unexperienced life is not worth living."

Adventurous Free Spirits like to live in the moment and can be impulsive. As kids, they may get into trouble when they act before thinking things through or considering the consequences of their actions. (Remembering your own childhood, you may even recall saying to yourself, "Well, it seemed like a good idea at the time.") Understanding your child's desire to capture the thrill can help you encourage their adventurousness while at the same time keeping them safe. For all children, the frontal lobe of the brain, specifically the prefrontal cortex, which is responsible for executive functions like reasoning and impulse control, typically doesn't finish developing until about age thirty. This may be especially true for Adventurous Free Spirits.

Finally, while you and your child share several strengths, you may also share similar blind spots. Both of you tend to think quite logically but are not naturally introspective or comfortable dealing with feelings and emotions. If you ever feel impatient when your child is expressing their feelings, it's important to remember that you've had decades of experience learning to understand your feelings and deal with them in a healthy way. But your child has not. So, it's important to make a point of consciously paying attention to how they are feeling and be willing to engage with them, even, and especially, when you find it uncomfortable to do so.

Having deep personal conversations that involve feelings is not one of most Adventurous Free Spirit parents' natural gifts. And yet it is an extremely important role you must play. It's possible that your partner may be more comfortable in this area than you. If this is the case, the Adventurous Free Spirit parent may learn some useful tips by listening to and watching that parent talk to their child.

When trying to engage your Adventurous Free Spirit child in a conversation, bear in mind that they are more likely to respond to specific questions, rooted in reality, rather than hypothetical ones that require them to use their imagination. For example, if your child was being bullied by a classmate and you ask them "What do you think Jason will do if you tell him he hurt your feelings?" you're likely to be met with a blank stare, followed by "I don't know." (Because they don't.) But if you ask them "Have you told Jason that he hurt your feelings?" followed by "What did he say (or do)?" you'll have a better chance of getting them to provide additional information that will help you have a more productive conversation.

With that said, here are:

Tried and true suggestions for engaging your
Adventurous Free Spirit

- Use fun activities and treats to reward positive behavior; turn chores into games and make them fun whenever possible.
- Recognize that they learn best by experiencing things firsthand.
- Teach them how to take reasonable risks, steering them to-

ward activities that excite, but aren't like to injure, them.
- Don't misinterpret a lack of overt affection as a lack of love and caing.
- Set crystal-clear boundaries, and show them what you mean, rather than simply telling them.

This information is provided for educational purposes only and is not meant to diagnose any condition, or explain or predict any future behavior or conditions in children or adults of any personality type, as each person is a unique individual.

CHAPTER 18
Adventurous Free Spirit Parent (Type 3)
& Gentle Humble Helper Child (Type 4)

Of course, you know your child better than anyone! But with some types of children, regardless of how diligent the parent is, it's almost impossible to know what's going on beneath the surface. This Parent/Child Profile provides important new insights into your child, yourself, and how your similarities and differences affect your interactions, all with an eye toward helping you build the healthiest, most fulfilling relationship possible.

Your personality type:

Adventurous Free Spirit
Seize the Day!

Adventurous Free Spirits love to have fun and tend to not take things too seriously or sweat the small stuff. Rather than make plans too far in advance, they like to be free to be spontaneous and respond to whatever is happening in the moment. As a result, they can be impulsive and take more risks than others may be comfortable with.

Adventurous Free Spirits tend to be competitive and like winning, and they are usually not especially concerned about how those they defeat may feel about their loss. Many are quite physical, enjoying sports and being in nature. They also may like to take things apart to see how they work—and are usually able to put them back together. They cherish their freedom and don't like being micromanaged or told what to do; nor do they have difficulty bending the rules when that seems to them like a reasonable thing to do.

One finds Adventurous Free Spirits in all occupations, but they

often gravitate to work that affords them a lot of freedom and excitement, that includes physical activity, a variety of tasks, and the opportunity to use specific skills they've mastered, and that doesn't require excessive supervision. Some fields that often attract people of this type include being a first responder (police officer, firefighter, EMT), athletic coach, sports commentator, builder, trial attorney, tradesperson, surgeon, or stock trader.

Adventurous Free Spirits represent about 18% of the population.

Your child's personality type:

Gentle Humble Helper
Practice random acts of kindness.

Gentle Humble Helpers tend to be easy-going, warm, kind-hearted, and modest. They are very sensitive and feel things deeply but are likely to share their feelings only with people they trust. These are kids who like to please others and avoid conflict at all costs. They are usually very loyal friends who are good at sharing their toys and possessions.

Gentle Humble Helpers are natural nurturers. They usually get great pleasure from helping others, especially younger children, and are often drawn to and fond of caring for animals. These are fairly realistic kids, and so their play often tends to be more physical, like playing sports, climbing trees, and playing hide-and-seek, rather than engaging in word games or making up imaginary scenarios.

Gentle Humble Helpers usually have a good sense of humor, but if they make jokes, it is seldom at anyone else's expense. They like being spontaneous and responding to what comes up rather than making plans for the future. They can also be impulsive, doing things that seem like a good idea…at the time.

Gentle Humble Helpers represent only about 9% of the population, making them the rarest of the five personality types.

How you're similar to and different from your child

In general, the more similar two people's personality types, the easier, though not necessarily better, the relationship. Three similarities and differences have the greatest impact: how people perceive the world, their core motivators, and their preferred communication style.

You may find that you and your child are similar in some ways, but different in other ways.

An important similarity is that both Adventurous Free Spirit parents and their Gentle Humble Helper children both take in information primarily through their five senses, which tends to make them realistic and practical, focusing on what is happening in the moment, not what might happen in the future. For example, your high-school-junior son decides to take an easier course so he can play sports, not factoring in how this might affect his chances of getting into his first-choice college next year.

Another important difference is in your varied motivators, which often determine the behaviors and activities that give you the greatest satisfaction. Most Adventurous Free Spirits derive their greatest satisfaction from being free to simply be present and enjoy their lives with as few rules and people telling them what to do as possible, whereas your Gentle Humble Helper child likely derives their greatest satisfaction from helping people in real and practical ways. As an example, you may encourage your daughter to go to law school so she'll have a secure financial future, but she loves working with kids and wants to teach elementary school, even though she won't make as much money.

An important advantage in your relationship is that you and your child both have the same temperament—the innate qualities that influence a person's values and key motivators. Words most often used to describe Adventurous Free Spirits are fun-loving, risk-taking, spontaneous, active, adaptable, and impulsive. While similar in many ways, adjectives that best describe Gentle Humble Helpers are caring, kind, nurturing, spontaneous, and adaptable.

Another component describes the different ways your two types communicate and prefer to be communicated with. In many ways, your communication styles are quite similar.

Both Adventurous Free Spirits and Gentle Humble Helpers communicate in a direct, straightforward manner, preferring to talk about practical realities rather than abstract ideas. As a result, they seldom have a hard time understanding what the other is saying. Although their style is similar, what they choose to talk about can be quite different. Because Adventurous Free Spirits tend to be quite logical and analytical, they usually focus on more impersonal things and situations, whereas the more sensitive

Gentle Humble Helpers may talk more about people, or sometimes animals, to which they are often drawn.

How this may play out in your relationship

All parents want what's best for their kids. Often, mostly unconsciously, parents believe their children will be happier and more successful by being more like them. But what happens when your child is very different from you?

Many child psychologists believe that the happiest, healthiest children are those whose parents really understand and appreciate them for the unique individuals they are. This is what fosters self-esteem. Of course, the opposite is also true: when children are not seen for who they are or appreciated and celebrated for their gifts, they often grow up not feeling good about themselves—or not good enough, in general.

Both Adventurous Free Spirit parents and their Gentle Humble Helper children have what is known as kinesthetic intelligence: they're usually good at using their bodies to express themselves, learn, and solve problems. They're often adept at physical activities and learn best through hands-on experiences, so they are often drawn to sports and enjoy being in nature.

The greatest difference between the two of you are the criteria you use to make most of your decisions. Adventurous Free Spirits tend to be more logical and objective, while Gentle Humble Helpers make more of their decisions based on how they feel about something and how they and others will be affected by their decisions. This is a significant difference, one that is very important for parents of these children to understand.

Gentle Humble Helpers are both extremely sensitive and often uncomfortable sharing their feelings with others, even their parents. Unlike their Adventurous Free Spirit parents, who usually let most things roll off their backs, Gentle Humble Helpers tend to take things personally. For example, Adventurous Free Spirits often enjoy teasing others and may like playing practical jokes. They don't do this to be hurtful! They do it because they think it's funny and believe others will feel the same way. But they are simply not hard-wired to sense how the other person may feel about the experience. Even gentle ribbing can make the Gentle Humble Helper feel uncomfortable. And because they're not confrontational, the "offender" may never hear about the discomfort they caused.

Potential vulnerabilities

Although every individual is unique, research shows that many Gentle Humble Helpers have a higher-than-average risk of developing anxiety and depression and may be more susceptible to others' negative online behavior. But every individual is unique. Therefore, this does not mean that your child is necessarily at increased or decreased risk.

How to nurture your child

"Meet your child where they are." Great advice: easy to give, and much harder to do! Stretching outside of one's comfort zone is hard and may take some practice, especially when the parent's and child's personality types are very different. But it is no less important than making sure your child is safe, clothed, or fed and may be more critical to protecting their mental health and promoting their wellbeing.

We all have gifts that make us special, for which we want to be appreciated and celebrated. As an Adventurous Free Spirit, among your greatest is your ability to be in the moment, to keenly observe what's happening around you, enjoy whatever you're doing, and help others to as well. You'll probably take it as a compliment if someone were to say "You are so much fun! I always have such a good time when I'm with you!" In contrast, saying the same thing to a Gentle Humble Helper would not mean nearly as much as if they said "Thank you so much! Your thoughtfulness means more to me than you can imagine."

Having deep personal conversations that involve feelings is not one of most Adventurous Free Spirits parents' natural gifts. And yet it is an extremely important role you must play. It's possible that if your partner is a Feeler, they're probably more comfortable dealing with emotions. If this is the case, the Adventurous Free Spirit parent may learn some useful tips by listening to and watching that parent talk to their child.

When trying to engage your Gentle Humble Helper child in a conversation, they are more likely to respond to specific questions, rooted in reality, rather than hypothetical ones that require them to use their imagination. For example, if you ask them "What do you think Jason will do if you tell him he hurt your feelings?," you're likely to be met with a blank stare, followed by "I don't know." (Because they don't.) But if you ask them "Have you told Jason that he hurt your feelings?" followed by "What did he say (or do)?," you'll have a better chance of getting them to provide additional information that will help you have a more productive conversation.

With that said, here are:

Tried and true suggestions for engaging your Gentle Humble Helper:

- Smile, give them lots of hugs and kisses, and frequently tell them you love them.
- Give them very specific directions and instructions and show them what you mean whenever possible.
- Accept their need to be physically active. Play with them and surprise them; be spontaneous.
- Support their feelings and allow them to express them in their own time and style.
- Use incentives and rewards that are tangible, such as fun activities, freedom, money, and treats.

This information is provided for educational purposes only and is not meant to diagnose any condition, or explain or predict any future behavior or conditions in children or adults of any personality type, as each person is a unique individual.

CHAPTER 19
Adventurous Free Spirit Parent (Type 3) & Creative Sensitive Soul Child (Type 5)

Of course, you know your child better than anyone! But with some types of children, regardless of how diligent the parent is, it's almost impossible to know what's going on beneath the surface. This Parent/Child Profile provides important new insights into your child, yourself, and how your similarities and differences affect your interactions, all with an eye toward helping you build the healthiest, most fulfilling relationship possible.

Your personality type:

Adventurous Free Spirit
Seize the Day!

Adventurous Free Spirits love to have fun and tend to not take things too seriously or sweat the small stuff. Rather than make plans too far in advance, they like to be free to be spontaneous and respond to whatever is happening in the moment. As a result, they can be impulsive and take more risks than others may be comfortable with.

Adventurous Free Spirits tend to be competitive and like winning, and they are usually not especially concerned about how those they defeat may feel about their loss. Many are quite physical, enjoying sports and being in nature. They also may like to take things apart to see how they work—and are usually able to put them back together. They cherish their freedom and don't like being micromanaged or told what to do; nor do they have difficulty bending the rules when that seems to them like a reasonable thing to do.

One finds Adventurous Free Spirits in all occupations, but they

often gravitate to work that affords them a lot of freedom and excitement, that includes physical activity, a variety of tasks, and the opportunity to use specific skills they've mastered, and that doesn't require excessive supervision. Some fields that often attract people of this type include being a first responder (police officer, firefighter, EMT), athletic coach, sports commentator, builder, trial attorney, tradesperson, surgeon, or stock trader.

Adventurous Free Spirits represent about 18% of the population.

Your child's personality type:

Creative Sensitive Soul
Seeing possibilities everywhere.

Creative Sensitive Souls feel things deeply and are very empathetic. As a result, they avoid conflict and try to make people happy, often putting others' needs ahead of their own. Because these children often feel things more intensely than other types of children, they can feel lonely and sometimes sense that they don't quite belong.

Because Creative Sensitive Souls have vivid imaginations and feel things so deeply, they are the most idealistic of all the types. They know the way things should be (but seldom are), which can cause them to become moody, disillusioned, or depressed. Usually loving and physically affectionate, they may also be easily frightened and prone to worrying.

Many Creative Sensitive Souls are, as their name implies, creative, which they may express through art, music, poetry, dance, acting, and other such endeavors. They often have vivid imaginations, and when they're young they may like to play games that begin with "Let's pretend..." They tend to take things personally and can be moody and easily upset when criticized.

Creative Sensitive Souls represent about 17% of the population.

How you're similar to and different from your child

In general, the more similar two people's personality types, the easier, though not necessarily better, the relationship. Three similarities and differences have the greatest impact: how people perceive the world, their core motivators, and their preferred communication style.

You probably find that you and your child are very different types of people. There may even be times when you've asked yourself where did this child come from? Because of your different hard-wiring and the unique nature of Creative Sensitive Souls, it is especially important for you to understand those differences.

The first difference is how the two of you prefer to take in information. Adventurous Free Spirits do this primarily through their five senses, which tends to make them realistic, practical, and down to earth. They pay attention to what's happening in the moment rather than what they imagine might happen sometime in the future.

But Creative Sensitive Souls experience the world very differently, relying on their intuition or sixth sense to take in information, focusing less on what is than what is possible, what something means, and how it is connected to other things. These children see possibilities everywhere! Another way to look at this is that Adventurous Free Spirits focus on the details and specifics and take most things at face value, while Creative Sensitive Souls naturally see the big picture and easily connect the dots. For example, your science-loving son is very worried about how global warming endangers many species, but you believe that the climate is constantly changing and don't see any point in worrying about something that might or might not happen sometime in the future.

Another important difference is in what motivates the two of you, which often influences your behaviors and interests. Most Adventurous Free Spirits derive their greatest satisfaction from being free to simply be present and enjoy their lives with as few rules and people telling them what to do as possible. They love to be able to respond spontaneously when a fun activity presents itself.

In contrast, Creative Sensitive Souls derive great satisfaction from coming up with creative solutions to people's problems. As an example, even in high school, friends of Creative Sensitive Souls often turn to them for relationship advice, often commenting that they would make a good psychologist. (In fact, there are significantly more Creative Sensitive Soul therapists than one would expect to find, given their percentage of the general population.)

Another significant difference is that these two types also have different temperaments, innate qualities that are often considered the core of one's personality type and that influence their values, competencies, and interests. Some words most used to describe

Adventurous Free Spirits such as you are fun-loving, risk-taking, spontaneous, active, adaptable, and impulsive, while adjectives most often used to describe your **Creative Sensitive Soul** child are empathetic, idealist, perceptive, creative, spiritual, compassionate, and collaborative.

Another difference is how the two of you communicate and prefer to be communicated with. **Creative Sensitive Souls** are very empathetic and perceptive about how others are feeling and instinctively want to make them feel good. They are also much more likely to take even mild and constructive criticism personally. **Adventurous Free Spirits** tend to communicate in a direct, straightforward manner, preferring to talk about practical realities rather than abstract ideas, and because they are quite logical and analytic by nature, they usually provide honest, if sometimes blunt and undiplomatic, feedback. For example, in an effort to be helpful, you may tell your son who just struck out that his batting stance is all wrong. But what he hears is that he's not good enough and has disappointed you.

How this may play out in your relationship

All parents want what's best for their kids. Often, mostly unconsciously, parents believe their children will be happier and more successful by being more like them. But what happens when your child is very different from you?

Many child psychologists believe that the happiest, healthiest children are those whose parents really understand and appreciate them for the unique individuals they are. This is what fosters self-esteem. Of course, the opposite is also true: when children are not seen for who they are or appreciated and celebrated for their gifts, they often grow up not feeling good about themselves—or not good enough, in general.

Parents of **Creative Sensitive Soul** children like yours need to understand that every feeling is valid. parents tend to view feelings and emotions very differently. For example, if their child's friend is hurt in a car accident, then it makes sense to them for their child to be upset or scared, and the parent will recognize the need to comfort their child. But if their daughter has not been invited to the party of a classmate that she really doesn't like but nevertheless has had her feelings hurt by not being invited, the **Adventurous Free Spirit** parent might be inclined to dismiss how she feels, perhaps saying something like "I don't understand why this is such a big deal. I thought you didn't like her." Although the parent is trying to be helpful, the child might take this as a criticism that she's too sensitive.

Adventurous Free Spirit parents like to make things fun and are good at doing so. They're also prone to teasing and often enjoy playing practical jokes. But because their Creative Sensitive Soul child tends to take things personally, they can easily get their feelings hurt, leaving the parent to wonder "What just happened?" Because Creative Sensitive Soul children are so sensitive, and their parents typically are not, the parent may be inclined to tell their child to just lighten up! But to the child this can feel dismissive and hurtful.

Finally, many Creative Sensitive Soul children tend to be creative and drawn to the arts, acting in plays, taking dance lessons, attending writing workshops, and going to museums, whereas many Adventurous Free Spirit parents are drawn to physical activities such as participating in or watching sports, hiking, and camping. The trick for these parents is to support their child's natural interests and desires while at the same time broadening their interests by exposing them to physical activities, perhaps playing a team sport that can provide them with important life lessons.

Potential vulnerabilities

Although every individual is unique, research shows that Creative Sensitive Souls may be at significantly higher risk of developing anxiety and depression and more susceptible to bullying and others' negative online behavior. With these children, it's especially important to constantly monitor how they are feeling, because they have deep feelings but don't often share them. That said, every individual is unique. Therefore, this does not mean that your child is necessarily at increased or decreased risk for depression, anxiety, or bullying.

How to nurture your child

"Meet your child where they are." Great advice: easy to give, and much harder to do! Stretching outside of one's comfort zone is hard and may take some practice, especially when the parent's and child's personality types are very different. But it is no less important than making sure your child is safe, clothed, or fed and may be more critical to protecting their mental health and promoting their wellbeing.

We all have gifts that make us special, for which we want to be appreciated and celebrated. As an Adventurous Free Spirit, among your greatest gifts are your ability to be in the moment, keenly observe what's going on around you, enjoy whatever you're doing, and help others to as well. You'll probably take it as a compliment if someone were to say "You are so much fun! I always have a good time when I'm with you!"

But your Creative Sensitive Soul child's greatest gifts are very different and likely include their empathy and desire to make a positive difference in others' lives. Recognizing and appreciating your child's greatest gifts lets them know that you see and love them for who they are. And although empathy is certainly a wonderful quality to have, it can also lead these naturally idealistic types of kids to become anxious or depressed as they recognize that many things are not as they could or should be.

Every combination of a parent's and child's personality types presents unique opportunities and challenges. This is especially true for the Adventurous Free Spirit parent who has a Creative Sensitive Soul child. Simply stated, what your child needs most, your deep understanding of and willingness to explore and discuss their feelings, simply does not come naturally to most people of your personality type. Does this mean that you are incapable of providing this level of support? Absolutely not! Only that it will take a little extra work on your part. But it will pay huge dividends in the future.

It's possible that your partner or another care giver finds nurturing your child this way comes more naturally. If this is the case, you may learn how to do this better yourself by listening to and observing how they interact with your child.

Your Creative Sensitive Soul child probably has a rich imagination, which they enjoy using. So asking them to help brainstorm solutions to a problem they share with you (especially if they're more extraverted) is more likely to get them engaged, and you're likely to learn more about what's going on in their life, as well.

With that said, here are:

Tried and true suggestions for engaging your Creative Sensitive Soul:

- Try not to judge or rush them through their feelings.
- Appreciate their individuality and express your love and

affection frequently.
- Forgive them quickly and never give them the silent treatment.
- Encourage them to speak their truth and not sugarcoat things.
- Listen to and support their ideas; don't squelch their creativity or originality.

This information is provided for educational purposes only and is not meant to diagnose any condition, or explain or predict any future behavior or conditions in children or adults of any personality type, as each person is a unique individual.

Gentle Humble Helper Parent

and their Child Personality Types

CHAPTER 20
Gentle Humble Helper Parent (Type 4)
& Responsible Hard Worker Child (Type 1)

Of course, you know your child better than anyone! But with some types of children, regardless of how diligent the parent is, it's almost impossible to know what's going on beneath the surface. This Parent/Child Profile provides important new insights into your child, yourself, and how your similarities and differences affect your interactions, all with an eye toward helping you build the healthiest, most fulfilling relationship possible.

Your personality type:

Gentle Humble Helper
Practice random acts of kindness.

Gentle Humble Helpers tend to be easy-going, warm, kind, and nurturing. They are very sensitive and feel things deeply but are likely to share their feelings only with people they trust. Realistic and practical, they tend to avoid conflict at all costs and like to please others, sometimes putting others' needs ahead of their own.

Gentle Humble Helpers are playful and usually have a good sense of humor, but if they make a joke, it is seldom at someone else's expense. They like being spontaneous, responding to what comes up rather than making plans, especially far into the future. They can also be impulsive, doing things that seem like a good idea…at the time.

One finds Gentle Humble Helpers in all occupations, but they often gravitate to work that affords them a lot of freedom and flexibility and a casual, tension-free environment in which they get to help people or animals in real and practical ways. Specific fields

that often attract people of this type include healthcare, EMT work, massage, physical and occupational therapy, and caring for children, adults, and animals.

Gentle Humble Helpers represent only about 9% of the population, making them the rarest of the five personality types.

Your child's personality type:

Responsible Hard Worker
Always do the right thing

Your child's personality type: Responsible Hard Worker
Always trying to do the right thing.

Responsible Hard Workers tend to be serious and cautious. They like familiar routines and traditions. By their nature, they like structure and boundaries and tend to follow the rules, and they expect others to follow them, too.

As children and adolescents, Responsible Hard Workers are usually not especially challenging to parent. They tend to be fairly compliant when it comes to doing their chores, finishing their homework, and helping out with younger siblings. They usually take their responsibilities, such as caring for their pets, seriously.

Responsible Hard Workers usually respect authority figures such as parents, teachers, doctors, and police officers, and they don't tend to push the envelope or rock the boat. They have a strong sense of duty and often feel an obligation to help others. They're most comfortable when plans have been made and can get upset when plans are changed, especially at the last minute. They are usually driven to finish whatever they start, such as games, art projects, or puzzles.

Responsible Hard Workers represent about 46% of the population, making them the most common personality type.

How you're similar to and different from your child

In general, the more similar two people's personality types, the easier, though not necessarily better, the relationship. Three similarities and differences have the greatest impact: how people perceive the world, their core motivators, and their preferred communication style.

It's probably no surprise that in some ways, you and your child are quite different. One very important characteristic you share is that both Gentle Humble Helpers like you and your Responsible Hard Worker child take in information primarily through your five senses, which tends to make you both pretty realistic, practical, and down to earth. You focus more on what is happening in the moment than what might occur in the future.

Gentle Humble Helpers derive their greatest satisfaction from being present, responsive, and flexible and helping people in real and concrete ways. In contrast, among the things that give Responsible Hard Workers the greatest satisfaction is taking on a task and completing it. For example, while you might have put off cleaning out the garage for months, your Responsible Hard Worker child may enjoy taking it on, especially if they're complimented and compensated for doing a good job.

One of the most significant differences between these two types is what is called their temperament, the innate qualities that influence a person's values and key motivators. Words that are most often used to describe Gentle Humble Helpers' temperament are sensitive, fun-loving, humble, nurturing, adaptable, helpful, and cooperative. In contrast, adjectives often used to describe your Responsible Hard Worker child's temperament are dependable, organized, productive, service-oriented, trustworthy, traditional, and consistent.

Another key difference between your and your child's types is whether you have more of a play or work ethic. Because Gentle Humble Helpers often prioritize enjoyment, they may be tempted to drop what they're doing (especially if it's an arduous task) if some fun opportunity presents itself. This doesn't mean they don't get their work done, only that they may put it off until a later time to seize the moment. This is seldom the case with Responsible Hard Workers, who are driven to complete what they start and are seldom guilty of procrastination (especially in older children).

In terms of their communication style, both types tend to be straightforward and concise and prefer to talk about real things rather than abstract ideas or concepts. It's likely, then, that while you and your child may not always agree, you shouldn't find it hard to understand where the other is coming from.

How this may play out in your relationship

All parents want what's best for their kids. Often, mostly unconsciously, parents believe their children will be happier and more successful by being more like them. But what happens when your child is very different from you?

Many child psychologists believe that the happiest, healthiest children are those whose parents really understand and appreciate them for the unique individuals they are. This is what fosters self-esteem. Of course, the opposite is also true: when children are not seen for who they are or appreciated and celebrated for their gifts, they often grow up not feeling good about themselves—or not good enough, in general.

Without getting too deep into the weeds, there's something else you need to know about Gentle Humble Helpers. They are Feeling types, which means they make decisions primarily based on their values and how they and others will be affected by their actions. But Responsible Hard Workers come in two varieties: Some are also Feelers, and some are Thinkers who make most decisions primarily based on logic and impersonal analysis. What makes sense to them is usually more important than how others may feel about or be affected by their decision or action. For example, your 11-year-old Thinking Responsible Hard Workers daughter was seemingly unaware of how her teasing was upsetting her younger cousin, and it was hard for you to get her to apologize. Empathy is not something that comes naturally to Thinkers, especially to younger children.

Why is it important to know if your child is a Thinker or a Feeler? Because if your Responsible Hard Worker child is a Feeler, they are much more likely to need your emotional support and be more willing to discuss their feelings with you. If, however, they are a Thinker, they will probably be much less comfortable sharing their feelings, even with their parents. And all children have big feelings they need to process with a trusted adult.

Because Gentle Humble Helpers are playful and spontaneous by nature and Responsible Hard Workers are more serious and planful, there may be times when you might be tempted to tell your child to lighten up. But for these responsible, serious souls, this well-intentioned suggestion may feel like criticism and make them feel that you don't really understand them.

Responsible Hard Worker children tend to love traditions and familiar routines and can become anxious when plans are changed, especially at the last minute. As an example, your family has vacationed at the same spot for many years, but this year you've decided to try a new place, and your child is having a hard time adjusting to the change.

Responsible Hard Worker children also tend to take people literally and expect others, especially their parents, to do what they say they will and when they say they will do it. This is why your daughter may get very upset if you are 15 minutes late picking her up from soccer practice.

Potential vulnerabilities

Although every individual is unique, research shows that most **Responsible Hard Workers** have a much lower-than-average risk of developing anxiety and depression. This is especially true if your child is a Thinker, but less so if they are a Feeler. Similarly, a Thinker child may also be less susceptible to bullying and negative online behavior than a Feeling child. But because every individual is unique, this does not mean that your child is necessarily at an increased or decreased risk for anxiety, depression, or the effects of bullying.

How to nurture your child

"Meet your child where they are." Great advice: easy to give, and much harder to do! Stretching outside of one's comfort zone is hard and may take some practice, especially when the parent's and child's personality types are very different. But it is no less important than making sure your child is safe, clothed, or fed and may be more critical to protecting their mental health and promoting their wellbeing.

We all have gifts that make us special and for which we want and need to be appreciated. As a **Gentle Humble Helper,** among the things you probably value most about yourself are your kindness, loyalty, ability to be present in the moment, and desire to always be helpful.

But among your **Responsible Hard Worker** child's greatest gifts are their strong work ethic, desire to follow the rules and be productive, and for others to know they can be counted on to do whatever they say they will do. Recognizing and appreciating your child's greatest gifts lets them know that you see and love them for who they are.

As discussed above, you will probably have an easier time relating to your **Responsible Hard Worker** child if they are a Feeler, like you. But if they are a Thinker, it may be more challenging, and you will need to choose your words carefully to get them to open up to you and not make them feel uncomfortable and shut down.

Fortunately for your child, Gentle Humble Helper parents like you usually are high in emotional intelligence, making you the perfect person to help your children develop healthy ways of dealing with their feelings. But because you are so sensitive and crave a harmonious relationship with your child, you may avoid uncomfortable but necessary conversations for fear they may lead to conflict.

When trying to engage your Responsible Hard Worker child in a conversation, they are more likely to respond to specific questions rooted in reality, rather than hypothetical ones that require them to use their imagination. For example, if you ask them "What do you think Jason will do if you tell him he hurt your feelings?" you're likely to be met with a blank stare, followed by "I don't know." (Because they don't.) But if you ask them "Have you told Jason that he hurt your feelings?" followed by "What did he say (or do)?" you'll have a better chance of getting them to provide additional information that will help you have a more productive conversation.

Tried and true suggestions for engaging your
Responsible Hard Worker:

- Be clear and explicit in your directions and requests: say what you mean and mean what you say.
- Prepare them in advance for new experiences and changes in plans.
- Be on time; follow through on all your commitments to them.
- Encourage them to question things, rather than always taking things at face value.
- Reward them with increasing levels of responsibility and praise them for their accomplishments.

This information is provided for educational purposes only and is not meant to diagnose any condition, or explain or predict any future behavior or conditions in children or adults of any personality type, as each person is a unique individual.

CHAPTER 21
Gentle Humble Helper Parent (Type 4)
& Strategic Problem Solver Child (Type 2)

Of course, you know your child better than anyone! But with some types of children, regardless of how diligent the parent is, it's almost impossible to know what's going on beneath the surface. This Parent/Child Profile provides important new insights into your child, yourself, and how your similarities and differences affect your interactions, all with an eye toward helping you build the healthiest, most fulfilling relationship possible.

Your personality type:

Gentle Humble Helper
Practice random acts of kindness.

Gentle Humble Helpers tend to be easy-going, warm, kind, and nurturing. They are very sensitive and feel things deeply but are likely to share their feelings only with people they trust. Realistic and practical, they tend to avoid conflict at all costs and like to please others, sometimes putting others' needs ahead of their own.

Gentle Humble Helpers are playful and usually have a good sense of humor, but if they make a joke, it is seldom at someone else's expense. They like being spontaneous, responding to what comes up rather than making plans, especially far into the future. They can also be impulsive, doing things that seem like a good idea…at the time.

One finds Gentle Humble Helpers in all occupations, but they often gravitate to work that affords them a lot of freedom and flexibility and a casual, tension-free environment in which they get to help people or animals in real and practical ways. Specific fields that often attract people of this type include healthcare, EMT work, massage, physical and occupational therapy, and caring for children, adults, and animals.

Gentle Humble Helpers represent only about 9% of the population, making them the rarest of the five personality types.

Your child's personality type:

Strategic Problem Solver
Everything can be improved.

Your child's personality type: Strategic Problem Solvers
Everything can be improved.

Strategic Problem Solvers tend to be independent, strong-willed, and competitive. Their thirst for knowledge and love of learning drives them to excel and often results in their being high achievers. Their thought process can be complex, and they connect most dots quite easily. As a result, they love to figure things out and find ways to improve upon them, and they are usually gifted at doing so.

Strategic Problem Solvers can be challenging to parent because they often like to argue or push back, especially when something doesn't make sense or seems unfair to them. Because they're driven to be the best, they're usually good at whatever interests them, but they can become bored if they're not adequately challenged. They usually come across as confident and self-assured but may also appear somewhat aloof, and they often don't show affection easily. Logical and analytical, Strategic Problem Solvers are often very objective and don't tend to take things personally.

Strategic Problem Solvers represent only about 10% of the population, making them one of the rarest personality types.

How you're similar to and different from your child

In general, the more similar two people's personality types, the easier, though not necessarily better, the relationship. Three similarities and differences have the greatest impact: how people perceive the world, their core motivators, and their preferred communication style.

It's probably no surprise that you and your child are quite different.

Gentle Humble Helpers take in information primarily through their five senses, which tends to make them realistic and practical. They focus on what is happening in the moment, not what might be in the future. For them, the world is not a terribly complicated place.

Strategic Problem Solvers rely heavily on their intuition or sixth sense to take in information, focusing less on what is than what's possible, what something means and how it is connected to other things and issues.

Gentle Humble Helpers derive their greatest satisfaction from helping people in real and concrete ways. In contrast, most Strategic Problem Solvers are most motivated by being successful, which they achieve by being lifelong learners and constantly challenging themselves to develop new competencies. They are more interested in and talented at solving big problems that affect lots of people rather than taking a more personal approach and helping individuals.

One of the most significant differences between these two types is what is called their temperament, the innate qualities that influence a person's values and key motivators. Words that are most often used to describe Gentle Humble Helpers' temperament are sensitive, fun-loving, humble, nurturing, adaptable, helpful, and cooperative. In contrast, adjectives often used to describe your Strategic Problem Solver child's temperament are competent, confident, independent, assertive, intellectual, strategic, high achieving, and competitive.

When it comes to communication, Gentle Humble Helpers tend to be straightforward and concise and like to talk about real things and people rather than novel ideas or concepts. Strategic Problem Solvers' communication style is quite different. They usually love talking about ideas, and their conversations often include lots of seemingly random thoughts linked together. As a result, Gentle Humble Helpers may find them unclear and confusing. By contrast, Strategic Problem Solvers sometimes worry that Gentle Humble Helpers can get so mired in the details they fail to see the big picture, nuances, or implications of what the conversation is really all about.

How this may play out in your relationship

All parents want what's best for their kids. Often, mostly unconsciously, parents believe their children will be happier and more successful by being more like them. But what happens when your child is very different from you?

Many child psychologists believe that the happiest, healthiest children are those whose parents really understand and appreciate them for the unique individuals they are. This is what fosters self-esteem. Of course, the opposite is also true: when children are not seen for who they are or appreciated and celebrated for their gifts, they often grow up not feeling good about themselves—or not good enough, in general.

Gentle Humble Helpers are very nurturing people, tuned in to how others are feeling, especially those they love, and eager to make them feel good—one of their most central needs. But when they are unable to help someone in need, it can make them feel helpless and anxious. Typically, their Strategic Problem Solver child is not nearly as sensitive as they are, often not in touch with how they feel, tend to discount the importance of feelings, in general, and seldom see the benefit of sharing theirs. This very fundamental difference can be equally frustrating for the parent and child.

Along with being sensitive, Gentle Humble Helpers also tend to love giving and receiving physical affection. However, Strategic Problem Solver children seldom have the same level of need, which can leave the parent feeling rejected and having their feelings hurt. For example, a Gentle Humble Helper woman dreamed of having a baby girl, frequently fantasizing about the emotionally intimate relationship they would share. But almost from day one, and true to her child's nature, her beautiful Strategic Problem Solver baby girl never wanted or engaged in the kind of physical affection the mom craved. It was almost impossible for the mom to not unconsciously send her daughter the message "you're not good enough"—in this case, not affectionate enough.

Understanding early on that her daughter simply had very different innate needs than the mom's could have served both the mother and daughter well and might have resulted in the healthiest, most loving intimate relationship, which is what the mother wanted all along.

Finally, Strategic Problem Solvers are very often high achievers. While Gentle Humble Helper parents certainly want their children to succeed, they may question, openly or secrety, their child's priorities. As an example, the parent may get upset if the child prefers to attend a science fair rather than participate in a family dinner or reunion.

Potential vulnerabilities

Although every individual is unique, research shows that most Strategic Problem Solvers have a lower-than-average risk of developing anxiety and depression and may be less susceptible to others' bullying and other negative online behavior. But every individual is unique. Therefore, this does not mean that your child is necessarily at increased or decreased risk.

How to nurture your child

"Meet your child where they are." Great advice: easy to give, and much harder to do! Stretching outside of one's comfort zone is hard and may take some practice, especially when the parent's and child's personality types are very different. But it is no less important than making sure your child is safe, clothed, or fed and may be more critical to protecting their mental health and promoting their wellbeing.

We all have gifts that make us special, for which we want and need to be appreciated. As a Gentle Humble Helper, among the things you probably value most about yourself are your kindness, loyalty, and desire to always be helpful.

But your Strategic Problem Solver has very different gifts, which include a quick and agile mind, intellectual curiosity, and the ability to be logical and objective and to quickly grasp complex ideas and concepts. They are often high academic achievers and love learning. Recognizing and appreciating them for these gifts and competencies lets your child know that you see and love them for who they are, especially if they are very different from you.

A special word to Gentle Humble Helper parents: You may find it especially challenging to get your Strategic Problem Solver child to share how they are feeling with you, for a couple of reasons. First, their brains process information much more logically and analytically than yours. So, for all their brilliance in other areas, they are seldom gifted in emotional intelligence, the ability to recognize, understand, and manage emotions in oneself and others. People who are high in emotional intelligence often have heightened self-awareness, empathy, and social skills, which are crucial for building strong relationships. Second, they often don't recognize the value or importance of the emotional world. That said, all children are constantly experiencing and need to learn to process deep feelings. Fortunately for them, Gentle Humble Helper parents are usually high in emotional intelligence, putting you in the perfect position to help your children develop healthy ways of dealing with their feelings.

Your Strategic Problem Solver child probably has a rich imagination, which they enjoy using. So, asking them to help brainstorm solutions to a problem they share with you (especially if they're more extraverted) is more likely to get them engaged, and you're likely to learn more about what's going on in their life, as well.

With that said, here are:

Tried and true suggestions for engaging your
Strategic Problem Solver:
- Compliment them on teir creative ideas and logical arguments and be willing to let them win.
- Model open and honest communication of feelings; help them develop kindness, generosity, and tact.
- Expect to be challenged and respect their strong need for independence.
- Be fair and consistent in discipline; explain the logical, rational reasons for decisions and rules.
- Try not to take a lack of overt affection on their part personally and find common interests to foster closeness and intimacy.
- Reward them with increasing levels of responsibility and praise them for their accomplishments.

This information is provided for educational purposes only and is not meant to diagnose any condition, or explain or predict any future behavior or conditions in children or adults of any personality type, as each person is a unique individual.

CHAPTER 22
Gentle Humble Helper Parent (Type 4) & Adventurous Free Spirit Child (Type 3)

Of course, you know your child better than anyone! But with some types of children, regardless of how diligent the parent is, it's almost impossible to know what's going on beneath the surface. This Parent/Child Profile provides important new insights into your child, yourself, and how your similarities and differences affect your interactions, all with an eye toward helping you build the healthiest, most fulfilling relationship possible.

Your personality type:

Gentle Humble Helper
Practice random acts of kindness.

Gentle Humble Helpers tend to be easy-going, warm, kind, and nurturing. They are very sensitive and feel things deeply but are likely to share their feelings only with people they trust. Realistic and practical, they tend to avoid conflict at all costs and like to please others, sometimes putting others' needs ahead of their own.

Gentle Humble Helpers are playful and usually have a good sense of humor, but if they make a joke, it is seldom at someone else's expense. They like being spontaneous, responding to what comes up rather than making plans, especially far into the future. They can also be impulsive, doing things that seem like a good idea...at the time.

One finds Gentle Humble Helpers in all occupations, but they often gravitate to work that affords them a lot of freedom and flexibility and a casual, tension-free environment in which they get to help people or animals in real and practical ways. Specific fields

that often attract people of this type include healthcare, EMT work, massage, physical and occupational therapy, and caring for children, adults, and animals.

Gentle Humble Helpers represent only about 9% of the population, making them the rarest of the five personality types.

Your child's personality type:

Adventurous Free Spirit
Seize the day!

Adventurous Free Spirits love to have fun and tend to not take things too seriously. Rather than make plans in advance, they prefer to be spontaneous and respond to whatever is happening in the moment. As a result, they can be impulsive and take more risks than their parents are comfortable with. Adventurous Free Spirits learn best by doing, rather than by reading or listening to a lecture. The more physical and tactile the experience, the more lasting impression it will leave on this type of child.

Many Adventurous Free Spirits are naturally competitive, like to win, and tend to not be especially concerned about how the person they defeat feels about their loss. Most of these kids are also quite physical, enjoying sports and being in nature. They also may like to take things apart to see how they work and can usually figure out how to put them back together again. They don't like being told what to do and are not opposed to bending the rules if they think they think they can get away with it. These children can also be impulsive, often doing things that seem like a good idea…at the time.

Adventurous Free Spirits represent about 18% of the population.

How you're similar to and different from your child

In general, the more similar two people's personality types, the easier, though not necessarily better, the relationship. Three similarities and differences have the greatest impact: how people perceive the world, their core motivators, and their preferred communication style.

In many ways, you and your child are quite similar. In other ways, you are quite different.

One very important thing you share is that you both take in information the same way: primarily through your five senses, which tends to make you realistic, practical, and down to earth. Parents and children of both types focus on what is happening in the moment, not what might occur in the future.

An important advantage in your relationship is that you and your child both share the same temperament, the innate qualities that influence a person's values and key motivators. Words most often used to describe Gentle Humble Helpers like you are caring, kind, nurturing, spontaneous, and adaptable. While similar in many ways, your Adventurous Free Spirit child is often described as fun-loving, risk-taking, spontaneous, active, adaptable, and impulsive.

But there is one significant difference: Gentle Humble Helpers are very sensitive souls whose greatest satisfaction comes from helping people in real and concrete ways. While playful, most enjoy the physicality or social aspect of a game, with winning usually being less important.

In contrast, most Adventurous Free Spirits derive their greatest satisfaction from living in the moment and enjoying their lives with as few restrictions as possible. Because they're usually not nearly as sensitive or take things as personally as Gentle Humble Helpers, they typically have a much more casual, playful demeanor, a "don't worry, be happy" approach to life. And they tend to be quite competitive. For example, a Gentle Humble Helper playing a game with a younger sibling is much more likely to let them win than an Adventurous Free Spirit might be in a similar situation.

When it comes to communication, Gentle Humble Helpers and Adventurous Free Spirits have a similar style and tend to be straightforward and concise and prefer to talk about real things rather than ideas or concepts. The greatest difference may be what they like to talk about. Gentle Humble Helpers' discussions frequently involve people, something they experienced and how they felt about it, whereas Adventurous Free Spirits usually prefer to talk about things, activities, or situations.

How this may play out in your relationship

All parents want what's best for their kids. Often, mostly unconsciously, parents believe their children will be happier and more successful by being more like them. But what happens when your child is very different from you?

Many child psychologists believe that the happiest, healthiest children are those whose parents really understand and appreciate them for the unique individuals they are. This is what fosters self-esteem. Of course, the opposite is also true: when children are not seen for who they are or appreciated and celebrated for their gifts, they often grow up not feeling good about themselves—or not good enough, in general.

Gentle Humble Helpers are very nurturing people, naturally tuned in to how others are feeling, especially those they love, and eager to make them feel good, which satisfies one of their most central needs. But when they are unable to help someone in need, it can make them feel helpless and anxious.

Their Adventurous Free Spirit child is likely not nearly as sensitive, seldom in touch with how they feel, and tends to discount the importance of feelings, failing to see the need for or benefit of sharing them with parents or others. This very fundamental difference can be equally frustrating for parents and children of this personality type combination.

As well as being sensitive, Gentle Humble Helpers also tend to love to give and receive physical affection. However, few Adventurous Free Spirit children have the same level of need, which can result in the parent's feeling rejected and having their feelings hurt. For example, a Gentle Humble Helper woman dreamed of having a baby girl, frequently fantasizing about the emotionally intimate relationship they would share. But almost from day one, and true to her child's nature, her beautiful Adventurous Free Spirit baby girl never wanted or engaged in the kind of physical affection the mom craved. It was almost impossible for the mom to not unconsciously send her daughter the message "you're not good enough"—in this case, not affectionate enough.

Understanding early on that her daughter simply had very different innate needs than her own could have served both the mother and daughter well and might have resulted in the healthiest, most loving intimate relationship, which is what the mother wanted all along.

Finally, while Gentle Humble Helpers and Adventurous Free Spirits have similar strengths, they may also have similar blind spots. For example, neither type naturally tends to be especially organized or particularly time conscious. However, everyone has to get to places on time, finish homework and other assignments, and so forth.

This can be a challenge for parents of Adventurous Free Spirits and may require them to come up with compensatory strategies, such as waking their children up earlier than they'd like to make sure they're not late for school, posting (and filling in!) a calendar on their refrigerator, or plastering Post-it note reminders around the house.

Potential vulnerabilities

Although every individual is unique, research shows that most Adventurous Free Spirits have a slightly higher-than-average risk of developing anxiety and depression but are probably not more susceptible to others' bullying and other negative online behavior. But because every individual is unique, this does not mean that your child is necessarily at increased or decreased risk.

How to nurture your child

"Meet your child where they are." Great advice: easy to give, and much harder to do! Stretching outside of one's comfort zone is hard and may take some practice, especially when the parent's and child's personality types are very different. But it is no less important than making sure your child is safe, clothed, or fed and may be more critical to protecting their mental health and promoting their wellbeing.

We all have gifts that make us special, for which we want and need to be appreciated. As a Gentle Humble Helper, among the things you probably value most about yourself are your kindness, loyalty, ability to be present in the moment, and desire to always be helpful.

But what your Adventurous Free Spirit child may value most about themself is their ability to be present and responsive to whatever is happening in the moment. Recognizing and appreciating your child's greatest gifts lets them know that you see and love them for who they are.

A special word to Gentle Humble Helper parents: You may find it especially challenging to get your Adventurous Free Spirit child to share how they are feeling with you, for a couple of reasons. First, their brains process information much more logically and analytically than yours does. So they are often not very high on emotional intelligence, the ability to recognize, understand, and manage emotions in themselves and others. In contrast, people who are high in emotional intelligence often have heightened self-awareness, empathy, and social skills, which helps them build strong, satisfying relationships. Second, they often don't recognize the value or importance of the emotional world. That said, all children are constantly experiencing and need to learn to process deep feelings. Fortunately for them, Gentle Humble Helper parents usually are high in emotional intelligence, making you the perfect person to help your child develop healthy ways of dealing with their feelings.

When trying to engage your Adventurous Free Spirit child in a conversation, they are more likely to respond to specific questions rooted in reality, rather than hypothetical ones that require them to use their imagination. For example, if you ask them "What do you think Jason will do if you tell him he hurt your feelings," you're likely to be met with a blank stare, followed by "I don't know." (Because they don't.) But if you ask them "Have you told Jason that he hurt your feelings?" followed by "What did he say (or do)?" you'll have a better chance of getting them to provide additional information that will help you have a more productive conversation.

With that said, here are:

Tried and true suggestions for engaging your Adventurous Free Spirit:

- Use fun activities and treats to reward positive behavior; turn chores into games and make them fun whenever possible.
- Recognize that they learn best by experiencing things firsthand.
- Teach them how to take reasonable risks, steering them toward activities that excite, but aren't like to injure, them.
- Don't misinterpret a lack of overt affection as a lack of love and caring.
- Set crystal-clear boundaries, and show them what you mean, rather than simply telling them.

This information is provided for educational purposes only and is not meant to diagnose any condition, or explain or predict any future behavior or conditions in children or adults of any personality type, as each person is a unique individual.

CHAPTER 23
Gentle Humble Helper Parent & Child (Type 4)

Of course, you know your child better than anyone! But with some types of children, regardless of how diligent the parent is, it's almost impossible to know what's going on beneath the surface. This Parent/Child Profile provides important new insights into your child, yourself, and how your similarities and differences affect your interactions, all with an eye toward helping you build the healthiest, most fulfilling relationship possible.

It's relatively rare for children and parents to share the same personality type, but when they do, the two are usually similar in many ways. Personality is a combination of nature—your inborn personality type—and nurture—everything else you experience in life, the greatest influence being your parents. While you and your child may be kindred spirits in many ways, there will be profound differences between the two of you because every person is a unique individual and because of your different ages, generations, experiences, and, most importantly, who you were parented by.

Here is a snapshot of the personality type you share with your child. If after reading this report you think that you may have misidentified your own or your child's type, you may want to revisit Chapter 4.

Your and your child's personality type:

Gentle Humble Helper
Practice random acts of kindness.

Gentle Humble Helpers tend to be easy-going, warm, kind, and nurturing. They are very sensitive and feel things deeply but are likely to share their feelings only with people they trust. Realistic and practical, they tend to avoid conflict at all costs and like to please others, sometimes putting others' needs ahead of their own.

Gentle Humble Helpers are playful and usually have a good sense of humor, but if they make a joke, it is seldom at someone else's expense. They like being spontaneous, responding to what comes up rather than making plans, especially far into the future. They can also be impulsive, doing things that seem like a good idea…at the time.

One finds Gentle Humble Helpers in all occupations, but they often gravitate to work that affords them a lot of freedom and flexibility and a casual, tension-free environment in which they get to help people or animals in real and practical ways. Specific fields that often attract people of this type include healthcare, EMT work, massage, physical and occupational therapy, and caring for children, adults, and animals.

Gentle Humble Helpers represent only about 9% of the population, making them the rarest of the five personality types.

Similarities with your child

In general, the more similar two people's personality types, the easier, though not necessarily better, the relationship. Three similarities and differences have the greatest impact: how people perceive the world, their core motivators, and their preferred communication style. The good news is that parents and children who are Gentle Humble Helpers generally perceive the world in the same way, taking in information primarily through their five senses, which tends to make them realistic, practical, and down to earth. They focus on what is happening in the moment, not what might occur in the future. For them, the world is not a terribly complicated place.

It's important for parents who share the same type with their child to remember that they may think like you, they may sound like you, they may even look like you—but they are not you. It's easy for some parents to think of their child as a "mini-me," which can be a source of tension.

When two people of the same type do experience conflict, it's often because they are too similar, having parallel weaknesses and blind spots. Weaknesses are things we know we're not good at, while blind spots are things we are unaware of that cause us to not be as effective as we'd like to be.

You may have noticed that it's not unusual to notice a personal quality or behavior in someone else that annoys you. Often, the reason is that we share that same quality but may not be aware of or able to own it. This can be even more prevalent when two people share the same personality type. It can feel like we're looking in the mirror—and don't necessarily like what we see.

For example, you and your child are both sensitive and caring and tend to be casual and laid-back. You both also have a strong instinctive drive for harmony, to make other people happy. While a lovely quality, this can also present challenges, which shows up when Gentle Humble Helpers become too invested in pleasing others and fail to ask for (or know) what they want or need. If they're not careful, this can lead to a co-dependent relationship, where one person has an unhealthy attachment to another person and such a strong need for their approval that they put the other person's needs ahead of their own. There's an old joke: two very nice people show up to a meeting at exactly the same time, but they never make it inside, because the one says, "You go first," and the other says, "No, you go first."

Gentle Humble Helpers often have similar interests and enjoy spending time together, especially when the child is young, but their laid-back approach to life may result in their not always getting things done, at least not on time. Of course, it's the parent's job to make the child toe the line, but that's not something that comes naturally to parents of this type. Being a disciplinarian is definitely not a role that most Gentle Humble Helpers relish!

Gentle Humble Helpers take in information primarily through their five senses. They focus on what is happening in the moment, not what might be in the future. This means that the two of you probably see the world in much the same way. And while you may not always agree, you should understand where the other person is coming from most of the time.

Gentle Humble Helpers derive great satisfaction from being present in the moment, responsive, flexible, and adaptable and helping people in real and practical ways.

When it comes to communication, Gentle Humble Helpers tend to be concise and straightforward and prefer to talk about real things and events, which almost always focus on people rather than on ideas or concepts, which is another important thing you share. While you may not always agree, you'll probably have no trouble understanding where the other person is coming from.

How this may play out in your relationship

All parents want what's best for their children. And often, mostly unconsciously, parents believe their children will be happier and more successful by being more like them.

Many child psychologists believe that the happiest, healthiest children are those whose parents really understand and appreciate them for the unique individuals they are. This is what fosters self-esteem. Of course, the opposite is also true: when children are not seen for who they are or appreciated and celebrated for their gifts, they often grow up not feeling good about themselves—or not good enough, in general.

Gentle Humble Helpers are very nurturing people, tuned in to how others are feeling, especially those they love, and eager to make them feel good, which satisfies one of their most central needs. But when they are unable to help someone in need, it can make them feel helpless and anxious.

It is generally a huge plus when a sensitive Gentle Humble Helper child has a sensitive and supportive parent who shares their personality type. But this shared sensitivity can also present challenges. Since they're both so invested in having a harmonious relationship, they tend to be people pleasers. This can show up in several ways, such as when both parent and child don't share unpleasant information with each other for fear of upsetting the other or don't ask for what they need. They can also be hypervigilant about how the other is feeling and find themselves walking on eggshells or taking on others' burdens as if they were their own. Parents and children who are both Gentle Humble Helpers may run the risk of developing a co-dependent relationship, one where there is excessive emotional or psychological reliance on the other person. More simply stated: one person often puts their own needs behind the other's.

Another unintended consequence is that Gentle Humble Helper children may not learn to trust a parent whom they sense, unconsciously, does not always tell them the truth for fear of upsetting them. However well-meaning it might be, not being truthful with your child can end up not only damaging your relationship but may also affect their future relationships with their partners, children, friends, and others

Potential vulnerabilities

Research shows that Gentle Humble Helpers have a higher-than-average risk of developing anxiety and depression and are likely to be more susceptible to others' bullying and other negative online behaviors. But because every individual is unique, this does not mean that your child is necessarily at increased or decreased risk.

How to nurture your child

"Meet your child where they are." Great advice: easy to give, and much harder to do! Stretching outside of one's comfort zone is hard and may take some practice, especially when the parent's and child's personality types are very different. But it is no less important than making sure your child is safe, clothed, or fed and may be more critical to protecting their mental health and promoting their wellbeing.

We all have gifts that make us special, for which we want and need to be appreciated. As a Gentle Humble Helper, among the things you probably value most about yourself are your kindness, loyalty, ability to be present in the moment, and desire to always be helpful. Your child values, or will in the future, these same qualities. You probably don't need to be reminded that it's critical for your child to feel free to express their feelings, good and bad. This can be a special challenge if your spouse's personality type is different from your and your child's, especially if they tend to be the tougher, more analytical type who is not naturally comfortable dealing with feelings and emotions. If this is the case, you can help your spouse be more effective by empathizing and modeling the kind of patient, loving support your child needs to thrive.

Finally, it's important for parents who share the same type with their child to remember that they may think like you, they may sound like you, they may even look like you—but they are not you. It's easy for some parents to think of their child as a "mini-me," which can cause conflict by setting up expectations that they will be and act more like you than they actually are.

When trying to engage your Gentle Humble Helper child in a conversation, they are more likely to respond to specific questions rooted in reality rather than hypothetical ones that require them to use their imagination. For example, if you ask them "What do you think Jason will do if you tell him he hurt your feelings?" you're likely to be met with a blank stare, followed by "I don't know." (Because they don't.) But if you ask them "Have you told Jason that he hurt your feelings?" followed by "What did he say (or do)?" you'll have a better chance of getting them to provide additional information that will help you have a more productive conversation.

It's important to keep in mind that all combinations of parent and child personality types have their joys (the easy stuff) and challenges (the tougher stuff). Parents who understand how their combination may predispose them to have a co-dependent relationship have a great advantage because they can take measures to ensure their child feels safe talking to them about everything!

That said, here are some:

Tried and true suggestions for engaging your
Gentle Humble Helper:

- Smile, give them lots of hugs and kisses, and frequently tell them you love them.
- Give them very specific directions and instructions and show them what you mean whenever possible.
- Accept their need to be physically active. Play with them and surprise them; be spontaneous.
- Support their feelings and allow them to express them in their own time and style.
- Use incentives and rewards that are tangible, such as fun activities, freedom, money, and treats.

This information is provided for educational purposes only and is not meant to diagnose any condition, or explain or predict any future behavior or conditions in children or adults of any personality type, as each person is a unique individual.

CHAPTER 24
Gentle Humble Helper Parent (Type 4) & Creative Sensitive Soul Child (Type 5)

Of course, you know your child better than anyone! But with some types of children, regardless of how diligent the parent is, it's almost impossible to know what's going on beneath the surface. This Parent/Child Profile provides important new insights into your child, yourself, and how your similarities and differences affect your interactions, all with an eye toward helping you build the healthiest, most fulfilling relationship possible.

Your personality type:

Gentle Humble Helper
Practice random acts of kindness.

Gentle Humble Helpers tend to be easy-going, warm, kind, and nurturing. They are very sensitive and feel things deeply but are likely to share their feelings only with people they trust. Realistic and practical, they tend to avoid conflict at all costs and like to please others, sometimes putting others' needs ahead of their own.

Gentle Humble Helpers are playful and usually have a good sense of humor, but if they make a joke, it is seldom at someone else's expense. They like being spontaneous, responding to what comes up rather than making plans, especially far into the future. They can also be impulsive, doing things that seem like a good idea…at the time.

One finds Gentle Humble Helpers in all occupations, but they often gravitate to work that affords them a lot of freedom and flexibility and a casual, tension-free environment in which they get to help people or animals in real and practical ways. Specific fields

that often attract people of this type include healthcare, EMT work, massage, physical and occupational therapy, and caring for children, adults, and animals.

Gentle Humble Helpers represent only about 9% of the population, making them the rarest of the five personality types.

Your child's personality type:

Creative Sensitive Soul
Seeing possibilities everywhere.

Creative Sensitive Souls feel things deeply and are very empathetic. As a result, they avoid conflict and try to make people happy, often putting others' needs ahead of themselves. Because these children often feel things more intensely than other types of children, they can feel lonely and sometimes sense that they don't quite belong.

Because Creative Sensitive Souls have vivid imaginations and feel things so deeply, they are the most idealistic of all the types. They know the way things should be (but seldom are), which can cause them to become moody, disillusioned, or depressed. Usually loving and physically affectionate, they may also be easily frightened and prone to worrying.

Many Creative Sensitive Souls are, as their name implies, creative, which they may express through art, music, poetry, dance, acting, and other such endeavors. They often have vivid imaginations, and when they're young they may like to play games that begin with "Let's pretend..." They tend to take things personally and can be moody and easily upset when criticized.

Creative Sensitive Souls represent about 17% of the population.

How you're similar to and different from your child

In general, the more similar two people's personality types, the easier, though not necessarily better, the relationship. Three similarities and differences have the greatest impact: how people perceive the world, their core motivators, and their preferred communication style. Gentle Humble Helpers take in information primarily through their five senses, which tends to make them realistic, practical, and down to earth. They mostly focus on what is happening in the moment rather than what might occur in the future.

But Creative Sensitive Souls experience the world very differently, relying on their intuition or sixth sense to take in information, focusing less on what is than what is possible, what something means and how it is connected to other things. They see possibilities everywhere! Another way to look at this is that you, as a Gentle Humble Helper, pay more attention to the details and specifics and tend to take things at face value. In contrast, your Creative Sensitive Soul child naturally tends to see the big picture, easily connects the dots, and has a vivid imagination and a rich inner life. As children, it is not unusual for them to have imaginary playmates, make up stories, and be drawn to things that are unusual. Gentle Humble Helpers are far more concrete and realistic. For example, when playing games with your child, they may want to make up their own rules or play with a toy in an entirely different way than it was intended. You may be tempted to correct the child for making a mistake, when in fact they just choose to do things differently from the way you might.

You and your child do share a very important inborn personality characteristic: you are both very sensitive and tuned into people's feelings, and you both get great satisfaction from helping others. People of both types are likely to take even mild criticism personally.

Gentle Humble Helpers derive their greatest satisfaction from being present in the moment, responsive, flexible, and adaptable and helping people in real and practical ways. In contrast, Creative Sensitive Souls derive great satisfaction from coming up with creative solutions to people's problems. As an example, even in high school, friends of Creative Sensitive Souls frequently turn to them for (mostly relationship) advice, often commenting that they would make a good psychologist. (In fact, there are significantly more Creative Sensitive Soul therapists than other types, based on their percentage in the population.)

When it comes to communication, Gentle Humble Helpers tend to be straightforward and concise, preferring to talk about real things and events, which almost always focus on people rather than more abstract ideas or concepts. Creative Sensitive Souls' communication style is more complex: a conversation may include lots of different thoughts presented in a seemingly random manner. Since they, older children especially, often love language, they may use metaphors and analogies and pepper their sentences with unusual words.

How this may play out in your relationship

All parents want what's best for their kids. Often, mostly unconsciously, parents believe their children will be happier and more successful by being more like them. But what happens when your child is very different from you?

Many child psychologists believe that the happiest, healthiest children are those whose parents really understand and appreciate them for the unique individuals they are. This is what fosters self-esteem. Of course, the opposite is also true: when children are not seen for who they are or appreciated and celebrated for their gifts, they often grow up not feeling good about themselves—or not good enough, in general.

Gentle Humble Helpers are very nurturing people, tuned in to how others are feeling, especially those they love, and eager to make them feel good, which satisfies one of their most central needs. But when they are unable to help someone in need, it can make them feel helpless and anxious.

It is generally a huge plus when a sensitive Creative Sensitive Soul child has a sensitive and supportive Gentle Humble Helper parent. But this shared sensitivity can also present challenges. Because both types are so invested in having a harmonious relationship, they tend to be people pleasers. This can show up in several ways, such as when both parent and child don't share unpleasant information for fear of upsetting the other, or not asking for what they need. Both can also be hypervigilant about how the other is feeling and take on their burdens as if they were their own. Parents and children of this type combination may run the risk of developing a co-dependent relationship, one where there is excessive emotional or psychological reliance on the other person. Simply stated, one person often puts their own needs behind the other's.

Another unintended consequence is that children may learn not to trust a parent whom they unconsciously sense may not always tell them the truth for fear of upsetting them. However well-meaning it might be, not being truthful with your child can end up not only damaging the parent-child relationship but affect their future relationships with their partners, children, friends, and others.

Potetial vulnerabilities

Research shows that Creative Sensitive Souls may have a significantly higher-than-average risk of developing anxiety and depression and are likely to be more susceptible to others' bullying and other negative online behavior. But because every individual is unique, this does not mean that your child is necessarily at increased or decreased risk.

How to nurture your child

"Meet your child where they are." Great advice: easy to give, and much harder to do! Stretching outside of one's comfort zone is hard and may take some practice, especially when the parent's and child's personality types are very different. But it is no less important than making sure your child is safe, clothed, or fed and may be more critical to protecting their mental health and promoting their wellbeing.

We all have gifts that make us special, for which we want and need to be appreciated. As a Gentle Humble Helper, among the things you probably value most about yourself are your kindness, loyalty, ability to be present in the moment, and desire to always be helpful.

But your Creative Sensitive Soul child's greatest gifts are very different: their empathy and desire to make a positive difference in others' lives. Recognizing and appreciating your child's greatest gifts lets them know that you see and love them for who they are. And although empathy is certainly a wonderful quality to have, it can also lead these naturally idealistic types of children to become anxious or depressed as they recognize that many things are not as they could or should be.

Many Creative Sensitive Soul children (and adults) tend to be worriers, because they can often imagine the worst-case scenario in almost any situation. This can be as simple as being afraid they won't be invited to a friend's party or as complicated as fearing that they have a serious medical condition, even though there's no evidence to suggest that they do. You can allay their fear by providing them with a reality check (something that comes naturally to you) in a gentle, reassuring way.

It's important to keep in mind that ALL combinations of parent and child personality types have their joys (the easy stuff) and challenges (the tougher stuff). Parents who understand how their particular combination may predispose them to have a co-dependent relationship have a great advantage because they can take measures to ensure their child feels safe talking to them about everything!

Your Creative Sensitive Soul child probably has a rich imagination, which they enjoy using. So, asking them to help brainstorm solutions to a problem they share with you (especially if they're more extraverted) is more likely to get them engaged, and you're likely to learn more about what's going on in their life, as well.

With that said, here are:

Tried and true suggestions for engaging your Creative Sensitive Soul:
- Try not to judge or rush them through their feelings.
- Appreciate their individuality and express your love and affection frequently.
- Forgive them quickly and never give them the silent treatment.
- Encourage them to speak their truth and not sugarcoat things.
- Listen to and support their ideas; don't squelch their creativity or originality.

This information is provided for educational purposes only and is not meant to diagnose any condition, or explain or predict any future behavior or conditions in children or adults of any personality type, as each person is a unique individual.

Creative Sensitive Soul Parent

and their Child Personality Types

CHAPTER 25
Creative Sensitive Soul Parent (Type 5) & Responsible Hard Worker Child (Type 1)

Of course, you know your child better than anyone! But with some types of children, regardless of how diligent the parent is, it's almost impossible to know what's going on beneath the surface. This Parent/Child Profile provides important new insights into your child, yourself, and how your similarities and differences affect your interactions, all with an eye toward helping you build the healthiest, most fulfilling relationship possible.

Your personality type:

Creative Sensitive Soul
Seeing possibilities everywhere.

Creative Sensitive Souls feel things deeply and are extremely empathetic. They typically avoid conflict and, in an effort to make people happy, can put others' needs ahead of their own. They tend to take things personally and can be moody and easily upset when criticized.

Creative Sensitive Souls usually have vivid imaginations and naturally see possibilities. Many are quite creative, expressing themselves through art, music, poetry, dance, acting, and other such outlets. Even as children, they can feel lonely because so few other people share their same values and deeply held beliefs. Usually loving and physically affectionate, they can be easily frightened and are prone to worrying.

One finds Creative Sensitive Souls in all occupations, but they often gravitate to work that involves helping people grow and develop their potential, makes use of their considerable creativity, and is in service of a mission in which they believe strongly. Specific

fields that attract many people of this type include psychology, counseling, teaching of the humanities, writing, producing, acting, journalism, and human resources.

Creative Sensitive Souls represent about 17% of the population.

Your child's personality type:

Responsible Hard Worker
Always trying to do the right thing.

Responsible Hard Workers tend to be serious and cautious. They like familiar routines and traditions. By their nature, they like structure and boundaries and tend to follow the rules, and they expect others to follow them, too.

As children and adolescents, Responsible Hard Workers are usually not especially challenging to parent. They tend to be compliant when it comes to doing their chores, finishing their homework, and helping with younger siblings. They usually take their responsibilities, such as caring for their pets, seriously.

Responsible Hard Workers usually respect authority figures such as parents, teachers, doctors, and police officers, and they don't tend to push the envelope or rock the boat. They have a strong sense of duty and often feel an obligation to help others. They're most comfortable when plans have been made and can get upset when plans are changed, especially at the last minute. They are usually driven to finish whatever they start, such as games, art projects, or puzzles.

Responsible Hard Workers represent about 46% of the population, making them the most common personality type.

How you're similar to and different from your child

In general, the more similar two people's personality types, the easier, though not necessarily better, the relationship. Three similarities and differences have the greatest impact: how people perceive the world, their core motivators, and their preferred communication style.

It's probably no surprise to you that you and your child are quite different: you're hard-wired to see the world very differently. Responsible Hard Workers take in information primarily through their five senses. They focus on their current reality, on what's happening in the moment, and not on what they imagine might happen sometime in the future. For example, your high school senior is filling out college applications but has no idea what he might want to study, or which career path he might want to pursue.

Creative Sensitive Souls' minds operate very differently. They rely heavily on their intuition or sixth sense to take in information, focusing less on what is than what something means and how it is connected to other things. The difference in how these two types perceive is quite fundamental, so it can lead to misunderstandings and is why they don't always appreciate the other's point of view.

Another important difference is in their varying motivators, which often determine the behaviors and activities that give them their greatest satisfaction. For most Creative Sensitive Souls their key driver is empathy, understanding people, and creating harmonious, meaningful relationships. They often take on causes and may work tirelessly to right a wrong or try to improve other peoples' lives.

Responsible Hard Workers, on the other hand, derive their greatest satisfaction from being of service in a real and tangible way, often in a traditional setting where there are clear expectations. For example, your daughter has made a commitment to tutor a younger child in math and meets with her each week at the same time. (And of course, you support her decisions!)

Another significant difference is that your two types also have different temperaments, often considered the core of one's personality type, which influence their values, competencies, and interests. Some words most used to describe Creative Sensitive Souls like you are empathetic, idealistic, perceptive, creative, spiritual, compassionate, and collaborative, whereas Responsible Hard Workers like your child are most often described as responsible, dependable, organized, hard-working, productive, and compliant.

Yet another component is the very different ways these two types communicate and prefer to be communicated with. Responsible Hard Workers tend to be straightforward and concise: "Say what you mean and mean what you say." They can find Creative Sensitive Souls unclear and confusing because Creative Sensitive Souls often link several different ideas in the same conversation and may jump around from one topic to another. For their part, Creative Sensitive Soul parents can get frustrated when their Responsible Hard Worker child seems to get so mired in the details that they fail to see the big picture and grasp what the conversation is really all about.

How this may play out in your relationship

All parents want what's best for their kids. Often, mostly unconsciously, parents believe their children will be happier and more successful by being more like them. But what happens when your child is very different from you?

Many child psychologists believe that the happiest, healthiest children are those whose parents really understand and appreciate them for the unique individuals they are. This is what fosters self-esteem. Of course, the opposite is also true: when children are not seen for who they are or appreciated and celebrated for their gifts, they often grow up not feeling good about themselves—or not good enough, in general.

As parents, Creative Sensitive Souls are very tuned into how their child is feeling, can usually sense if something's wrong, and love nothing better than a good heart-to-heart talk. But although some Responsible Hard Workers are more comfortable sharing their feelings, most are not. They may not even know how they're feeling or why, because their brains are not hard-wired to analyze things too deeply. This can be challenging for Creative Sensitive Soul parents who desperately want to help their child feel better but don't want them to get frustrated and shut down.

Another thing to keep in mind is that Creative Sensitive Souls are more prone than their Responsible Hard Worker offspring to suffer from anxiety and depression. It's possible that the Creative Sensitive Soul parent may project their own anxiety onto their child, when the child is just fine. In these instances, it might be helpful for the parent to get a reality check from a therapist or close friend who is more objective than you.

Finally, Responsible Hard Workers are planful creatures of habit. They like consistency, tend to be time-conscious, and expect people to do what they say they will do. For example, a Responsible Hard Worker child can become quite upset with their Creative Sensitive Soul parent if they are late picking the child up from school or athletic practice.

Potential vulnerabilities

Research shows that most Responsible Hard Workers have a lower-than-average risk of developing anxiety and depression and may be less susceptible to others' negative online behavior. But it's important to note there are two varieties of Responsible Hard

Workers: Thinkers tend to make most of their decisions based on logic, while Feelers base most of their decisions on how they feel about something and how they and others will be affected. Responsible Hard Workers who are Feelers may be more susceptible to anxiety, depression, and bullying than those who are Thinkers. But every individual is unique. Therefore, this does not mean that your child is necessarily at increased or decreased risk.

How to nurture your child

"Meet your child where they are." Great advice: easy to give, and much harder to do! Stretching outside of one's comfort zone is hard and may take some practice, especially when the parent's and child's personality types are very different. But it is no less important than making sure your child is safe, clothed, or fed and may be more critical to protecting their mental health and promoting their wellbeing.

We all have gifts that make us special, for which we want and need to be appreciated. As a Creative Sensitive Soul, you're probably proud of your abilities to understand and communicate with people, to see the big picture, and think outside the box. And you tend to see possibilities everywhere!

But your Responsible Hard Worker's greatest gifts, being realistic and practical, are just the opposite. They may see the creative but unconventional solutions you suggest as impractical, unworkable, and even wacky!

As described above, there are two varieties of Responsible Hard Worker children. Why is it important to know if your child is a Thinker or a Feeler? Because if your Responsible Hard Worker child is a Feeler, they are much more likely to need your emotional support and be more willing to discuss their feelings with you. If, however, they are a Thinker, they will probably be much less comfortable sharing their feelings, even with their parents. All children have big feelings they need to process with a trusted adult.

When trying to engage your Responsible Hard Worker child in a conversation, they are more likely to respond to specific questions, rooted in reality, rather than hypothetical ones that require them to use their imagination. For example, if you ask them "What do you think Jason will do if you tell him he hurt your feelings?" you're likely to be met with a blank stare, followed by "I don't know." (Because they don't.) But if you ask them "Have you told

Jason that he hurt your feelings?" followed by "What did he say (or do)?" you'll have a better chance of getting them to provide additional information that will help you have a more productive conversation.

With that said, here are:

Tried and true suggestions for engaging your Responsible Hard Worker:

- Be clear and explicit in your directions and requests; say what you mean and mean what you say.
- Prepare them in advance for new experiences and changes in plans.
- Recognize you both want to be, and often are, right. Learn to back off and to choose your battles.
- Be on time; follow through on all your commitments to them.
- Encourage them to question things rather than always taking things at face value.
- Reward them with increasing levels of responsibility and praise them for their accomplishments.

This information is provided for educational purposes only and is not meant to diagnose any condition, or explain or predict any future behavior or conditions in children or adults of any personality type, as each person is a unique individual.

CHAPTER 26
Creative Sensitive Soul Parent (Type 5)
& Strategic Problem Solver Child (Type 2)

Of course, you know your child better than anyone! But with some types of children, regardless of how diligent the parent is, it's almost impossible to know what's going on beneath the surface. This Parent/Child Profile provides important new insights into your child, yourself, and how your similarities and differences affect your interactions, all with an eye toward helping you build the healthiest, most fulfilling relationship possible.

Your personality type:
Creative Sensitive Soul
Seeing possibilities everywhere.

Creative Sensitive Souls feel things deeply and are extremely empathetic. They typically avoid conflict and, in an effort to make people happy, can put others' needs ahead of their own. They tend to take things personally and can be moody and easily upset when criticized.

Creative Sensitive Souls usually have vivid imaginations and naturally see possibilities. Many are quite creative, expressing themselves through art, music, poetry, dance, acting, and other such outlets. Even as children, they can feel lonely because so few other people share their same values and deeply held beliefs. Usually loving and physically affectionate, they can be easily frightened and are prone to worrying.

One finds Creative Sensitive Souls in all occupations, but they often gravitate to work that involves helping people grow and develop their potential, makes use of their considerable creativity, and is in service of a mission in which they believe strongly. Specific

fields that attract many people of this type include psychology, counseling, teaching of the humanities, writing, producing, acting, journalism, and human resources.

Creative Sensitive Souls represent about 17% of the population.

Your child's personality type:

Strategic Problem Solver
Everything can be improved.

Strategic Problem Solvers tend to be independent, strong-willed, and competitive. Their thirst for knowledge and love of learning drives them to excel and often results in their being high achievers. Their thought process can be complex, and they connect most dots quite easily. As a result, they love to figure things out and find ways to improve upon them, and they are usually gifted at doing so.

Strategic Problem Solvers can be challenging to parent because they often like to argue or push back, especially when something doesn't make sense or seems unfair to them. Because they're driven to be the best, they're usually good at whatever interests them, but they can become bored if they're not adequately challenged. They usually come across as confident and self-assured but may also appear somewhat aloof, and they often don't show affection easily. Logical and analytical, Strategic Problem Solvers are often very objective and don't tend to take things personally.

Strategic Problem Solvers represent only about 10% of the population, making them one of the rarest personality types.

How you're similar to and different from your child

In general, the more similar two people's personality types, the easier, though not necessarily better, the relationship. Three similarities and differences have the greatest impact: how people perceive the world, their core motivators, and their preferred communication style.

It's probably no surprise that you and your child are quite different. But in perhaps the most important way, you are quite similar. You both rely heavily on your intuition or sixth sense to take in information, focusing less on what is rather than on what's possible, what something means and how it is connected to other things. What this means in practical terms is that while you may not agree with one another's position or decisions, you should be able to understand where the other one is coming from.

Another important difference is in what motivates the two of you, which often influences the behaviors and activities that give you your greatest satisfaction. For Creative Sensitive Souls like you, this is being authentic and prioritizing having meaningful, harmonious relationships. They like solving problems on the personal level. Whereas most Strategic Problem Solvers like your child derive their greatest satisfaction from continuing to learn new things, develop new competencies, and be successful. They are fueled by solving problems on the less personal, macro level.

Creative Sensitive Souls often take on causes and work tirelessly to right a wrong or try to improve other people's lives. For example, in an argument about politics, you may both agree that the government has an important role to play. But being an empathetic Creative Sensitive Soul, you might feel the priority should be feeding poor people today, whereas your Strategic Problem Solver daughter may feel that taxpayers' dollars would be better spent improving the food delivery system that will benefit people someday in the future.

Your types also have different temperaments, often considered the core of one's personality type, which influence their values, competencies, and interests. Some words that are often used to describe Creative Sensitive Souls are empathetic, idealistic, perceptive, creative, spiritual, compassionate, and collaborative, while Strategic Problem Solvers are most often referred to as competent, confident, independent, intellectual, high achieving, and strategic.

Another component is the different ways these two types communicate and prefer to be communicated with.

Both Creative Sensitive Souls and Strategic Problem Solvers usually have very interesting conversations. Both like discussing big ideas, but what they like to talk about may be very different. Creative Sensitive Souls are people people who, as mentioned earlier, like intimate, deep, heart-to-heart conversations, whereas Strategic Problem Solvers almost always would prefer to talk about less-personal ideas rather than feelings, especially their own.

How this may play out in your relationship

All parents want what's best for their kids. Often, mostly unconsciously, parents believe their children will be happier and more successful by being more like them. But what happens when your child is very different from you?

Many child psychologists believe that the happiest, healthiest children are those whose parents really understand and appreciate them for the unique individuals they are. This is what fosters self-esteem. Of course, the opposite is also true: when children are not seen for who they are or appreciated and celebrated for their gifts, they often grow up not feeling good about themselves—or not good enough, in general.

As parents, Creative Sensitive Souls are very tuned into how their child is feeling, can usually sense if something's wrong and love nothing better than a good heart-to-heart talk. Strategic Problem Solvers are usually much less in touch with how they're feeling and find these conversations uncomfortable. This can be frustrating for Creative Sensitive Soul parents who desperately want to connect with and help a child who they think is struggling or unhappy. But at the same time, they don't want the child to shut down.

Another thing to keep in mind is that Creative Sensitive Souls tend to be worriers and much more prone than their Strategic Problem Solver offspring to suffer from anxiety and depression. Creative Sensitive Soul parents may unwittingly project their own anxiety onto their child when the child is, in fact, fine. In these instances, it might be helpful for the parent to get a reality check from a therapist or close friend who is more objective than they are.

Finally, Strategic Problem Solvers are very often high achievers. While Creative Sensitive Soul parents certainly want their children to succeed, they may question, openly or privately, their child's priorities. For example, your child may think it's more important to attend a science fair rather than participate in a family dinner or reunion.

Potential vulnerabilities

Research shows that Strategic Problem Solver children may have a lower-than-average risk of developing anxiety and depression and may be less susceptible to others' bullying and other negative online behavior. But every individual is unique. Therefore, this does not mean that your child is necessarily at increased or decreased risk.

How to nurture your child

"Meet your child where they are." Great advice: easy to give, and much harder to do! Stretching outside of one's comfort zone is hard and may take some practice, especially when the parent's and child's personality types are very different. But it is no less important than making sure your child is safe, clothed, or fed, and may be more critical to protecting their mental health and promoting their wellbeing.

We all have gifts that make us special, for which we want and need to be appreciated. As a Creative Sensitive Soul, among the things you probably value most about yourself are your empathy and perceptiveness about people, often referred to as emotional intelligence.

But your Strategic Problem Solver has very different gifts: a quick and agile mind, intellectual curiosity, and the ability to be logical and objective and to quickly grasp complex ideas and concepts. Recognizing and appreciating your child's gifts lets them know that you see and love them for who they are, especially if they are very different from you.

A special word to Creative Sensitive Soul parents: You may find it especially challenging to get your Strategic Problem Solver child to share how they are feeling with you, for a couple of reasons. First, their brains process information much more logically and analytically than yours. So, for all their brilliance in other areas, emotional intelligence, the ability to recognize, understand, and manage emotions in oneself and others, is seldom one of their strengths. People who are high in emotional intelligence like you often have heightened self-awareness, empathy, and social skills, which are crucial for building healthy relationships. Also, your Strategic Problem Solver child may not recognize the value or importance of the emotional world. That said, all children are constantly experiencing and need to learn to process deep feelings. Fortunately for them, Creative Sensitive Soul parents usually excel at this, making them the perfect person to help their children develop healthy ways of dealing with their feelings.

Although it might not seem to make intuitive sense, Creative Sensitive Souls tend to be either extremely optimistic, sometimes unrealistically so, or very pessimistic. Which one is truer for you may have a lot to do with the role models you had in your parents and how you were parented. Having this self-awareness can help make you an even more effective parent yourself.

Your Strategic Problem Solver child probably has a rich imagination, which they enjoy using. So asking them to help brainstorm solutions to a problem they share with you (especially if they're more extraverted) is more likely to get them engaged, and you're likely to learn more about what's going on in their life, as well.

With that said, here are:

Tried and true suggestions for engaging your Strategic Problem Solver:

- Compliment them on their creative ideas and logical arguments and be willing to let them win.
- Model open and honest communication of feelings; help them develop kindness, generosity, and tact.
- Expect to be challenged and respect their strong need for independence.
- Be fair and consistent in discipline; explain the logical, rational reasons for decisions and rules.
- Try not to take a lack of overt affection on their part personally and find common interests to foster closeness and intimacy.
- Reward them with increasing levels of responsibility and praise them for their accomplishments.

This information is provided for educational purposes only and is not meant to diagnose any condition, or explain or predict any future behavior or conditions in children or adults of any personality type, as each person is a unique individual.

CHAPTER 27
Creative Sensitive Soul Parent (Type 5) & Adventurous Free Spirit Child (Type 3)

Of course, you know your child better than anyone! But with some types of children, regardless of how diligent the parent is, it's almost impossible to know what's going on beneath the surface. This Parent/Child Profile provides important new insights into your child, yourself, and how your similarities and differences affect your interactions, all with an eye toward helping you build the healthiest, most fulfilling relationship possible.

Your personality type:

Creative Sensitive Soul
Seeing possibilities everywhere.

Creative Sensitive Souls feel things deeply and are extremely empathetic. They typically avoid conflict and, in an effort to make people happy, can put others' needs ahead of their own. They tend to take things personally and can be moody and easily upset when criticized.

Creative Sensitive Souls usually have vivid imaginations and naturally see possibilities. Many are quite creative, expressing themselves through art, music, poetry, dance, acting, and other such outlets. Even as children, they can feel lonely because so few other people share their same values and deeply held beliefs. Usually loving and physically affectionate, they can be easily frightened and are prone to worrying.

One finds Creative Sensitive Souls in all occupations, but they often gravitate to work that involves helping people grow and develop their potential, makes use of their considerable creativity, and is in service of a mission in which they believe strongly. Specific

fields that attract many people of this type include psychology, counseling, teaching of the humanities, writing, producing, acting, journalism, and human resources.

Creative Sensitive Souls represent about 17% of the population.

Your child's personality type:

Adventurous Free Spirit
Seize the day!

Adventurous Free Spirits love to have fun and tend to not take things too seriously. Rather than make plans in advance, they prefer to be spontaneous and respond to whatever is happening in the moment. As a result, they can be impulsive and take more risks than their parents are comfortable with. Adventurous Free Spirits learn best by doing, rather than by reading or listening to a lecture. The more physical and tactile the experience, the more lasting impression it will leave on these types of children.

Many Adventurous Free Spirits are naturally competitive, like to win, and tend to not be especially concerned about how the person they defeat feels about their loss. Most of these kids are quite physical, enjoying sports and being in nature. They also may like to take things apart to see how they work, and can usually figure out how to put them back together again. These are kids who don't like being told what to do and are not reluctant to bend the rules if they think they can get away with it. These children tend also to be impulsive and do things that seemed like a good idea…at the time.

Adventurous Free Spirits represent about 18% of the population.

How you're similar to and different from your child

In general, the more similar two people's personality types, the easier, though not necessarily better, the relationship. Three similarities and differences have the greatest impact: how people perceive the world, their core motivators, and their preferred communication style.

It's probably no surprise that you and your child are quite different: as a *Creative Sensitive Soul* you rely heavily on your sixth sense to take in information, focusing less on what is than why it is and how it is connected to other things. But your Adventurous Free Spirit child takes in information very differently, primarily through their five senses, focusing on what is happening in the moment, not what might be in the future. For example, your high school son decides to take an easier course so he can play sports, not factoring in how this might affect his chances of getting into his first-choice college. Being more future-oriented, you feel he should factor that into his decision.

Another important difference is in your varied motivators, which often determine the behaviors and activities that give you and your child their greatest satisfaction. For most Creative Sensitive Souls, this is being authentic and having meaningful, harmonious relationships, and their key drivers are empathy, understanding people, and helping them grow and develop. They often take on causes and may work tirelessly to right a wrong or try to improve other people's lives. They like solving problems on the personal level.

Most Adventurous Free Spirits derive their greatest satisfaction from being free to simply be present and enjoy their lives with as few restrictions, rules, and people telling them what to do as possible. They're often most comfortable in the physical world where they're actually doing something rather than in the intellectual world where they're thinking about or discussing something.

Another significant difference is that these two types also have different temperaments, often considered the core of one's personality type, which influence their values, competencies, and interests. Some words most used to describe Creative Sensitive Souls such as you are empathetic, idealist, perceptive, creative, spiritual, compassionate, and collaborative. Adventurous Free Spirits are most often described as fun-loving, risk taking, spontaneous, active, adaptable, and impulsive.

Yet another component is the different ways the two of you communicate and prefer to be communicated with. Creative Sensitive Souls love having deep, intimate conversations and are the most communicative of the five types. In sharp contrast, Adventurous Free Spirits are generally the least communicative, for a couple of reasons. Unlike Creative Sensitive Souls, they are not naturally introspective and tend to think more concretely than abstractly. Typically, they focus on what is happening in the moment, not necessarily on what it means. And they make decisions more objectively than personally. So, dealing with feelings, which are usually neither concrete or logical, is not something they enjoy or are comfortable with.

How this may play out in your relationship

All parents want what's best for their kids. Often, mostly unconsciously, parents believe their children will be happier and more successful by being more like them. But what happens when your child is very different from you?

Many child psychologists believe that the happiest, healthiest children are those whose parents really understand and appreciate them for the unique individuals they are. This is what fosters self-esteem. Of course, the opposite is also true: when children are not seen for who they are or appreciated and celebrated for their gifts, they often grow up not feeling good about themselves—or not good enough, in general.

As parents, Creative Sensitive Souls are very tuned into how their child is feeling, can usually sense if something's wrong, and love nothing better than a good heart-to-heart talk. They desperately want to connect with their child and help when they perceive they are unhappy or struggling. The challenge for these parents who have an Adventurous Free Spirit child is to gently get them to open up and to not make them feel so uncomfortable that their child shuts down and stops talking.

Because of how Creative Sensitive Souls' brains are hardwired, they tend to be more interested in intellectual pursuits than their Adventurous Free Spirit child, who often prefers more physical activities. There is actually a name for this: kinesthetic intelligence, which involves the capacity to manipulate objects and use a variety of physical skills. Athletes, dancers, and surgeons are among the people usually gifted in this way. For example, many Creative Sensitive Soul parents expect and encourage their Adventurous Free Spirit child to earn a college degree. But it is not uncommon for many of these children to prefer a career that is more physical or exciting, like being a first responder, a member of the military, or working in the trades.

Another thing to keep in mind is that Creative Sensitive Souls tend to be worriers and are more prone than their Adventurous Free Spirit child to suffer from anxiety and depression. Creative Sensitive Soul parents may unwittingly project their own anxiety onto their child when the child is, in fact, fine. In these instances, it might be helpful for the parent to get a reality check from a therapist or close friend who is more objective than they are.

Potential vulnerabilities

Research shows that Adventurous Free Spirits may have a slightly higher-than-average risk for anxiety and depression and may also be more affected by online bullying. But not all Adventurous Free Spirits are created equal, so some may be at even greater risk than others. Because every individual is unique, your child may not necessarily be at increased or decreased risk.

How to nurture your child

"Meet your child where they are." Great advice: easy to give, and much harder to do! Stretching outside of one's comfort zone is hard and may take some practice, especially when the parent's and child's personality types are very different. But it is no less important than making sure your child is safe, clothed, or fed, and may be more critical to protecting their mental health and promoting their wellbeing.

We all have gifts that make us special, for which we want and need to be appreciated. As a Creative Sensitive Soul, among the things you probably value most about yourself are your empathy and perceptiveness about people, which is often referred to as having high emotional intelligence.

But your Adventurous Free Spirit's gifts are quite different and may be hard for you to understand or appreciate. Many relate to the expression "la joie de vivre"— "the joy of living." Not only do they enjoy the moment, but they motivate others to, as well. They are also often very helpful in real and practical ways, such as assisting with physical chores or fixing things.

Finally, Adventurous Free Spirits can be adrenalin junkies, people who engage in high-risk activities because it gives them a rush. This can be especially challenging for Creative Sensitive Soul parents, who tend to be worriers. The trick for these types of parents with these types of kids is to let them do what they love to do (climb trees, perform tricks on skateboards, and the like), and keep them safe without undermining their confidence or making them unnecessarily fearful of taking reasonable risks.

A special word to Creative Sensitive Soul parents: Although it might seem counterintuitive, people of your type tend to be either extremely optimistic, sometimes unrealistically so, or very pessimistic and prone to anxiety or depression. Which one is truer for you may have a lot to do with the role models you had in your parents and how you were parented. Having this self-awareness can help make you an even more effective parent yourself.

When trying to engage your Adventurous Free Spirit child in a conversation, they are more likely to respond to specific questions rooted in reality rather than hypothetical ones that require them to use their imagination. For example, if you ask them "What do you think Jason will do if you tell him he hurt your feelings?" you're likely to be met with a blank stare, followed by "I don't know." (Because they don't.) But if you ask them "Have you told Jason that he hurt your feelings?" followed by "What did he say (or do)?," you'll have a better chance of getting them to provide additional information that will help you have a more productive conversation.

With that said, here are:

Tried and true suggestions for engaging your Adventurous Free Spirit:

- Use fun activities and treats to reward positive behavior; turn chores into games and make them fun whenever possible.
- Recognize that they learn best by experiencing things firsthand.
- Teach them how to take reasonable risks, steering them toward activities that excite, but aren't like to injure, them.
- Don't misinterpret a lack of overt affection as a lack of love and caring.
- Set crystal-clear boundaries, and show them what you mean, rather than simply telling them.

This information is provided for educational purposes only and is not meant to diagnose any condition, or explain or predict any future behavior or conditions in children or adults of any personality type, as each person is a unique individual.

CHAPTER 28
Creative Sensitive Soul Parent (Type 5) & Gentle Humble Helper Child (Type 4)

Of course, you know your child better than anyone! But with some types of children, regardless of how diligent the parent is, it's almost impossible to know what's going on beneath the surface. This Parent/Child Profile provides important new insights into your child, yourself, and how your similarities and differences affect your interactions, all with an eye toward helping you build the healthiest, most fulfilling relationship possible.

Your personality type:

Creative Sensitive Soul
Seeing possibilities everywhere.

Creative Sensitive Souls feel things deeply and are extremely empathetic. They typically avoid conflict and, in an effort to make people happy, can put others' needs ahead of their own. They tend to take things personally and can be moody and easily upset when criticized.

Creative Sensitive Souls usually have vivid imaginations and naturally see possibilities. Many are quite creative, expressing themselves through art, music, poetry, dance, acting, and other such outlets. Even as children, they can feel lonely because so few other people share their same values and deeply held beliefs. Usually loving and physically affectionate, they can be easily frightened and are prone to worrying.

One finds Creative Sensitive Souls in all occupations, but they often gravitate to work that involves helping people grow and develop their potential, makes use of their considerable creativity, and is in service of a mission in which they believe strongly. Specific

fields that attract many people of this type include psychology, counseling, teaching of the humanities, writing, producing, acting, journalism, and human resources.

Creative Sensitive Souls represent about 17% of the population.

Your child's personality type:

Gentle Humble Helper
Practice random acts of kindness

Gentle Humble Helpers tend to be easy-going, warm, kind-hearted, and modest. They are very sensitive and feel things deeply but are likely to share their feelings only with people they trust. These are kids who like to please others and avoid conflict at all costs. They are usually very loyal friends who are good at sharing their toys and possessions.

Gentle Humble Helpers are natural nurturers. They usually get great pleasure from helping others, especially younger children, and are often drawn to and fond of caring for animals. These are fairly realistic kids, and so their play often tends to be more physical, like playing sports, climbing trees, and playing hide-and-seek, rather than engaging in word games or making up imaginary scenarios.

Gentle Humble Helpers usually have a good sense of humor, but if they make jokes, it is seldom at anyone else's expense. They like being spontaneous and responding to what comes up rather than making plans for the future. They can also be impulsive, doing things that seem like a good idea…at the time.

Gentle Humble Helpers represent only about 9% of the population, making them the rarest of the five personality types.

How you're similar to and different from your child

In general, the more similar two people's personality types, the easier, though not necessarily better, the relationship. Three similarities and differences have the greatest impact: how people perceive the world, their core motivators, and their preferred communication style.

It's probably no surprise that you and your child are quite different: Creative Sensitive Souls rely heavily on their sixth sense to take in information, focusing less on what it is than why it is and how it is connected to other things, whereas your Gentle Humble Helper child takes in information primarily through their five senses. They focus on what is happening in the moment, not what might be in the future. For example, your son decides to take an easier course so he can play sports, not factoring in how this might affect his chances of getting into his first-choice college next year.

The difference in how these two types perceive can often lead to huge misunderstandings and explain why they don't always appreciate the other's point of view.

Another important difference is in their varying motivators, which often determine the behaviors and activities that give them their greatest satisfaction. For you as a Creative Sensitive Soul, this is probably being authentic and having meaningful, harmonious relationships. For most Creative Sensitive Souls the key drivers are empathy, understanding people, and helping them grow and develop. They often take on causes and may work tirelessly to right a wrong or try to improve other peoples' lives. They like solving problems on the personal level.

Gentle Humble Helpers, on the other hand, derive their greatest satisfaction from helping people in real and concrete ways. As an example, you encourage your daughter to go to law school so she'll have a secure financial future, but she loves working with kids and wants to teach elementary school, even though she won't make as much money.

Another significant difference is that these two types also have different temperaments, often considered to be the core of one's personality type, which influence their values, competencies, and interests. Some words most often used to describe Creative Sensitive Souls are empathetic, idealistic, perceptive, creative, spiritual, compassionate, and collaborative, whereas Gentle Humble Helpers are most often described as sensitive, easy-going, warm, playful, flexible, and nurturing.

Another component is the different ways these two types communicate and prefer to be communicated with. Creative Sensitive Souls love nothing more than deep intimate conversations and are the most communicative of the five types. In contrast, Gentle Humble Helpers are not naturally introspective and tend to think more concretely, focusing more on what is happening in the moment and not necessarily what it means or how it might affect them in the future. Despite this difference, a big advantage for parents and children of these two types is that both are sensitive and caring and genuinely want to be helpful to one another.

With regard to communication, Gentle Humble Helpers tend to be straightforward and concrete, preferring to talk about real things rather than more abstract ideas or concepts. But Creative Sensitive Souls' communication style is quite different. They love talking about ideas, especially new ones, and their conversations often include lots of ideas linked together. As a result, Gentle Humble Helpers may find them unclear and confusing. By contrast, Creative Sensitive Souls often feel that their child can get so mired in the weeds that they fail to see the big picture, nuances, or implications of what the conversation is really all about.

How this may play out in your relationship

All parents want what's best for their children. And often, mostly unconsciously, parents believe their children will be happier and more successful by being more like them. But what happens when one's child is very different from them?

Many child psychologists believe that the happiest, healthiest children are those whose parents really understand and appreciate them for the unique individuals they are. This is what fosters self-esteem. Of course, the opposite is also true: when children are not seen for who they are or appreciated and celebrated for their gifts, they often grow up not feeling good about themselves—or not good enough, in general.

As parents, Creative Sensitive Souls are very tuned into how their child is feeling, can usually sense if something's wrong, desperately want to help their child who may be struggling or unhappy, and believe that what can help best is a good heart-to-heart talk.

The challenge for these parents is that their Gentle Humble Helpers child often doesn't know the cause of what's bothering them. They may know they feel sad but don't understand why they do. To get their child to open up so the parent can fully understand the root of their child's unhappiness, the Creative Sensitive Soul parent needs to gently probe and be patient if it feels like their child is not forthcoming with information.

Because of how Creative Sensitive Souls' brains are wired, you tend to be more interested in intellectual pursuits than your Gentle Humble Helpers child, who often prefers more physical activities. Many of these children have what is called kinesthetic intelligence, which involves the capacity to manipulate objects and use a variety of physical skills. Athletes, dancers, and surgeons are among the people gifted in this way. For example, many Creative Sensitive Soul parents expect and encourage their Gentle Humble Helpers child to get a college degree. But it is not uncommon for these children to prefer a career that is more physical and nurturing, like working with children, the elderly, or animals, where they can be helpful in real and practical ways.

Another thing to keep in mind is that Creative Sensitive Souls tend to be worriers and suffer from anxiety or depression. Because Gentle Humble Helpers are very sensitive, Creative Sensitive Soul parents may unwittingly project their own anxiety onto their child when the child is, in fact, fine. Or the Creative Sensitive Soul parent may avoid talking to their child because they're afraid of what they might discover. In either case, it might be helpful for the parent to get a reality check from a therapist or close friend who is more objective than they are.

Potential vulnerabilities

Research shows that Gentle Humble Helpers have a higher-than-average risk for anxiety and depression and may also be more affected by online bullying. But not all Gentle Humble Helpers are created equal; some may be at even greater risk than others. However, because every individual is unique, your child may not necessarily be at increased or decreased risk.

How to nurture your child

"Meet your child where they are." Great advice: easy to give, and much harder to do! Stretching outside of one's comfort zone is hard and may take some practice, especially when the parent's and child's personality types are very different. But it is no less important than making sure your child is safe, clothed, or fed and may be more critical to protecting their mental health and promoting their wellbeing.

We all have gifts that make us special, for which we want and need to be appreciated. As a Creative Sensitive Soul, among the things you probably value most about yourself are your empathy and perceptiveness about people, which is often referred to as emotional intelligence.

But your *Gentle Humble Helper's* greatest gift is likely their ability to be a helpful, loyal friend, which is very different from yours! Recognizing and appreciating your child's greatest gifts lets them know that you see and love them for who they are.

A special word to *Creative Sensitive Soul* parents: Although it might seem counterintuitive, people of your type tend to be either extremely optimistic, sometimes unrealistically so, or very pessimistic and prone to anxiety or depression. Which one is truer for you may have a lot to do with the role models you had in your parents and how you were parented. Having this awareness can help you be an even more effective, nurturing parent yourself.

It's important to keep in mind that all combinations of parent and child personality types have their joys (the easy stuff) and challenges (the tougher stuff). Parents who understand how their combination may predispose them to have a co-dependent relationship have a great advantage because they can take measures to ensure their child feels safe talking to them about anything.

When trying to engage your *Gentle Humble Helper* child in a conversation, they are more likely to respond to specific questions rooted in reality rather than hypothetical ones that require them to use their imagination. For example, if you ask them "What do you think Jason will do if you tell him he hurt your feelings?" you're likely to be met with a blank stare, followed by "I don't know." (Because they don't.) But if you ask them "Have you told Jason that he hurt your feelings?" followed by "What did he say (or do)?" you'll have a better chance of getting them to provide additional information that will help you have a more productive conversation.

With that said, here are:

**Tried and true suggestions for engaging your
Gentle Humble Helper:**

- Smile, give them lots of hugs and kisses and often tell them you love them.
- Give them very specific directions and instructions: show them what you mean whenever possible.
- Accept their need to be physically active; play with them and surprise them; be spontaneous.
- Support their feelings and allow them to express them in

their own time and style.
- Use incentives and rewards that are tangible like fun, freedom, money, and treats.

This information is provided for educational purposes only and is not meant to diagnose any condition, or explain or predict any future behavior or conditions in children or adults of any personality type, as each person is a unique individual.

CHAPTER 29
Creative Sensitive Soul Parent & Child (Type 5)

Of course, you know your child better than anyone! But with some types of children, regardless of how diligent the parent is, it's almost impossible to know what's going on beneath the surface. This Parent/Child Profile provides important new insights into your child, yourself, and how your similarities and differences affect your interactions, all with an eye toward helping you build the healthiest, most fulfilling relationship possible.

It's relatively rare for children and parents to share the same personality type, but when they do, the two are usually similar in many ways. Personality is a combination of nature—your inborn personality type—and nurture—everything else you experience in life, the greatest influence being your parents. While you and your child may be kindred spirits in many ways, there will be profound differences between the two of you because every person is a unique individual and because of your different ages, generations, experiences, and, most importantly, who you were parented by.

Here is a snapshot of the personality type you share with your child. If after reading this report you think that you may have misidentified your own or your child's type, you may want to revisit Chapter 4.

Your and your child's personality type:

Creative Sensitive Soul
Seeing possibilities everywhere.

Creative Sensitive Souls are sensitive, feel things deeply, and, as young children, may be quick to cry. Extremely empathetic, they avoid conflict and try to make people happy, often putting others' needs ahead of their own. Many are creative, which they may express through art, music, poetry, dance, acting, and other endeavors.

Creative Sensitive Souls have vivid imaginations, and when they're young may like to start games with "Let's pretend... " They are likely to take things personally, can be moody, and are easily upset when criticized. Because these children often feel things more intensely than other types of children, they can feel lonely and sometimes sense that they don't quite belong. They are usually loving and physically affectionate, can be easily frightened, and are prone to worrying.

One finds Creative Sensitive Soul adults in all occupations, but they often gravitate to work that involves understanding and helping people grow and develop their potential, makes use of their creativity, and is in service of a mission in which they believe strongly. Specific fields that often attract people of this type include psychology, counseling, teaching of the humanities, the arts, writing, producing, acting, journalism, business, communication, human resources, marketing, and advertising.

Creative Sensitive Souls represent about 17% of the population.

Similarities with your child

In general, the more similar two people's personality types, the easier the relationship. Not necessarily better, but easier. A very consequential similarity is that both of you take in information in much the same way, relying on your intuition or sixth sense, which gives you a global perspective. Rather than focus on what it is, you naturally want to know why, connect the dots, see the big picture, and understand how things are related to one another. You also make decisions based on your strong values, feelings, and sensitivity to how you and others are affected by your actions.

Ironically, when two people of the same type do experience conflict, it's often because they are too similar, having similar weaknesses and blind spots. Weaknesses are things we know we're not good at, while blind spots are things we are unaware of that cause us to not be as effective as we'd like to be.

You may have noticed that it's not unusual to notice a personal quality or behavior in someone else that annoys you. Often, the reason is that we share that same quality but may not be aware of or able to own it. This can be even more prevalent when two people share the same personality type. It can feel like we're looking in the mirror—and don't necessarily like what we see.

For example, you and your child are both empathetic and quickly tune into how other people are feeling. You have an instinctive drive for harmony, to make people happy. While a lovely quality, this can also present challenges, which show up when Creative Sensitive Souls become too invested in making other people happy, sometimes to their own detriment. Creative Sensitive Souls are prone to co-dependence, which means they have an unhealthy attachment to another person and have such a strong need for their approval that they put the other person's needs ahead of their own.

Both you and your Creative Sensitive Soul child also have strong values that are usually, but not always, in harmony. This is especially true when children are younger and have not yet broken away in their quest for independence. The good news is that if a strong foundation has been built, they will often as adults embrace the values they learned as a child. It is also not uncommon for parents and children of this type to have some shared interests, especially regarding the arts, which may result in their both enjoying things like music, dance, writing, poetry, and painting.

Three of the most important components of personality type are the way people perceive the world, their core motivators, and their preferred communication style.

You both are hard-wired to share two key motivators that often influence the behaviors and activities that give you your greatest satisfaction: being authentic and having meaningful, harmonious relationships. Many Creative Sensitive Souls are drawn to causes and may work tirelessly to right a wrong or try to improve other people's lives. For example, even as a ten-year-old, your daughter may hear about a classmate who lost many of her possessions in a fire, and she decides to give that child several of her favorite toys and convinces her friends to do the same, a gesture that you of course wholeheartedly support and encourage.

Another helpful similarity is how Creative Sensitive Souls communicate and prefer to be communicated with. You both probably enjoy having interesting conversations. If one is more introverted and the other more extraverted, you may differ on the amount of discussion and how spontaneously you prefer it to take place.

How this may play out in your relationship

All parents want what's best for their children. And often, mostly unconsciously, parents believe their children will be happier and more successful by being more like them.

Many child psychologists believe that the happiest, healthiest children are those whose parents really understand and appreciate them for the unique individuals they are. This is what fosters self-esteem. Of course, the opposite is also true: when children are not seen for who they are or appreciated and celebrated for their gifts, they often grow up not feeling good about themselves—or not good enough, in general.

It's important for parents who share the same type with their child to remember that they may think like you, they may sound like you, they may even look like you—but they are not you. It's easy for some parents to think of their child as a "mini-me," which might create problems down the road.

Creative Sensitive Souls crave harmony, whether they're the parent or the child. As a result, either or both may avoid confronting the other for fear of upsetting them, which can have serious, long-term negative consequences, especially if a Creative Sensitive Soul learns that it's not safe to express their genuine feelings to a trusted adult.

A closely related challenge for Creative Sensitive Soul parents is that they tend to take many things personally, even when there's no reason to believe a comment or action was intended to be hurtful. This can even happen with their own child if, for example, the parent doesn't feel the child is being affectionate or loving enough. This can be especially trying during adolescence, when it's natural and healthy for the child to break away as they learn to be independent.

Additionally, Creative Sensitive Soul parents tend to be more overprotective than parents of the other types. This can be a very sensitive topic (and explains why few grandparents who have concerns about this issue raise them with their adult children!).

Most people will agree that a parent's first priority is to keep their child safe and healthy. But parents who protect their child from even having negative feelings can prevent that child from developing the critical life skill of resiliency, learning that they can be disappointed, angry, scared, hurt, or sad but get through that experience and be less affected by a similar one in the future.

Potential vulnerabilities

Research shows that Creative Sensitive Souls may have a significantly higher-than-average risk of developing anxiety and depression and are probably more susceptible to the effects of bullying and others' negative online behavior. But because every individual is unique, this does not mean that your child is necessarily at increased or decreased risk.

How to nurture your child

"Meet your child where they are." Great advice: easy to give, and much harder to do! Stretching outside of one's comfort zone is hard and may take some practice, especially when the parent's and child's personality types are very different. But it is no less important than making sure your child is safe, clothed, or fed and may be more critical to protecting their mental health and promoting their wellbeing.

We all have gifts that make us special, for which we want and need to be appreciated. As a Creative Sensitive Soul, among the things you probably value most about yourself are your empathy and perceptiveness about people, which is often referred to as emotional intelligence.

This quality can be a great advantage in raising your Creative Sensitive Soul child. It helps you recognize and appreciate your child's gifts, which lets your child know that you see and love them for who they are.

Another thing to keep in mind is that Creative Sensitive Souls tend to be worriers and often suffer from anxiety or depression, so parents of this type may unwittingly project their own anxiety onto their child when the child is, in fact, fine. Some Creative Sensitive Soul parents may avoid talking to their child because they're afraid of what they might discover. In either case, it might be helpful for the parent to get a reality check from a therapist or close friend who is more objective than they are.

A special word to Creative Sensitive Soul parents: Although it might seem counterintuitive, people of your type tend to be either extremely optimistic, sometimes unrealistically so, or very pessimistic and prone to anxiety or depression. Which one is truer for you may have a lot to do with the role models you had in your parents and how you were parented. Having this awareness can help you be an even more effective, nurturing parent yourself.

Your Creative Sensitive Soul child probably has a rich imagination, which they enjoy using. So asking them to help brainstorm solutions to a problem they share with you (especially if they're more extraverted) is more likely to get them engaged, and you're likely to learn more about what's going on in their life, as well.

With that said, here are:

Tried and true suggestions for engaging your Creative Sensitive Soul:
- Try not to judge or rush them through their feelings.
- Appreciate their individuality and express your love and affection frequently.
- Forgive them quickly and never give them the silent treatment.
- Encourage them to speak their truth and not feel they have to sugarcoat things.
- Listen to and support their ideas; don't squelch their creativity or originality.

This information is provided for educational purposes only and is not meant to diagnose any condition, or explain or predict any future behavior or conditions in children or adults of any personality type, as each person is a unique individual.

CHAPTER 30
A Vision for You

Final Thoughts, and a Reason to Be Hopeful
If you've read this far, you've likely done so with a mixture of determination and worry. Determination because you love your child deeply and want to do everything in your power to protect their mental health. Worry because you can see the difficult landscape our children are growing up in.

We cannot ignore the facts. In 2012, when smartphones became almost universal among teens, adolescent rates of anxiety, depression, and self-harm began to climb sharply. The data is sobering: since that time, major depressive episodes among adolescents have increased by more than 60% and anxiety disorders have followed a similar trajectory. The average teen now spends more than eight hours a day on screens, often replacing real-world play, physical activity, and face-to-face socializing with endless scrolling, gaming, and digital chatter. They are more connected than ever, yet more isolated than any generation before them.

This is, by any measure, a challenging time to be a parent—and to be a child. The pressures are relentless. Social media amplifies insecurities and creates unrealistic comparisons. Online platforms often prioritize outrage and drama because those keep users engaged. And all the while, opportunities for kids to just be kids—to roam a neighborhood with friends, to climb trees, to join pickup games at the park—have diminished dramatically.

Parents often tell me they feel powerless in the face of these cultural and technological forces. It can seem like we are swimming against a riptide. But here's the good news: you are not powerless. In fact, you have more influence than you may realize.

The Key is the Actual, Human Connection
The single most protective factor for your child's mental health is not the absence of social media, the perfect school, or even flaw-

less parenting. It is the presence of a strong, healthy, trusting relationship between you and your child. For your child to trust you and to come to you when they make a mistake. Or have a question. Or concern. Or fear.

Normalize talking about fears. Then help your children to separate real fears from imaginary ones. If you are steady and consistent, the bond between you will grow stronger over time.

When that bond is strong, your child is far more likely to share their worries, ask for help when they're struggling, and consider your guidance—even when they seem to push you away. That relationship becomes their anchor in a stormy sea.

And here's something equally important: a strong connection is not about agreeing on everything. It's not about eliminating conflict. It's about creating a foundation where disagreements don't erode trust and where your child believes—truly believes—that you are on their side, no matter what. Learn to speak to your child's personality type and allow for differences of opinion. Don't bludgeon, bully, or shame your children to be a mini-version of yourself. Each one of us has a unique spark. Talk to that spark in your child. Nurture it.

Throughout this book, we've talked about how to communicate with your child in ways they can understand, not just hear. That means knowing who your child is—their temperament, their personality, their sensitivities, and their strengths. When you understand how they are wired, you can predict the situations that might overwhelm them, the environments that might recharge them, and the ways in which they are most likely to feel supported.

In other words, you are learning to speak their language. And when you do that, your child feels seen, respected, and safe. Those three feelings—being seen, being respected, being safe—are the building blocks of resilience.

It's Time to Rehumanize Ourselves

To rehumanize ourselves is to reclaim the essence of our humanity that has been steadily eroded by digital addiction and the increasing presence of artificial intelligence in daily life. When we are constantly tethered to screens, we risk losing vital qualities that make us distinctly human: empathy, creativity, reflection, and the ability to be fully present with ourselves and with others.

Research shows that heavy reliance on digital technology—especially among young people—correlates with rising rates of loneliness, anxiety, and depression (Haidt, 2024). What was once considered normal human interaction, such as face-to-face conversation, playful outdoor activity, or the quiet act of reflection, has too often been replaced with scrolling, swiping, and algorithm-driven consumption. Rehumanizing ourselves is not merely a philosophical ideal; it is a practical call to action. It asks us to pause, step away from devices, and intentionally cultivate practices that restore our sense of dignity and worth beyond the digital world.

This process may begin with small but powerful acts: turning off one's phone for a designated portion of the day or even for a full "digital Sabbath" once a week (Turkle, 2015); scheduling nightly in-person check-ins with children or partners to foster authentic connection, or rediscovering the grounding influence of nature through a daily walk, gardening, or simply noticing the rhythms of the seasons. Studies have consistently shown that time spent in natural environments reduces stress and enhances psychological well-being (Bratman et al., 2019). Rehumanizing ourselves also involves reconnecting with our values—asking what truly matters apart from likes, views, and algorithmic validation—and choosing activities that reinforce intrinsic worth. These might include volunteering, practicing gratitude, or creating art for the joy of expression rather than for digital approval.

Ultimately, to rehumanize is to resist the normalization of constant connectivity and the illusion that speed and convenience are substitutes for meaning. It is important to remember that life is not lived best through screens but through presence, touch, laughter, and love. By reclaiming these practices, we repair the fractures created by our digital dependency and remind ourselves—and each other—that real life, in its deepest sense, happens offline.

Parenting in the Age of Distraction

Yes, the modern world makes parenting harder. You are competing for your child's attention against the most sophisticated attention-capturing technology ever invented. You are parenting in an age when the family dinner is often interrupted by a ping, a buzz, or a scroll, and when moments of boredom that once sparked creativity are now instantly filled with a screen.

But there is an upside to living in this era. We now have a better understanding than ever before of what helps children thrive—and what puts them at risk. We have data, neuroscience, and the lived experiences of millions of families that tell us exactly what works.

And here's the part that should give you hope: the things that work best have not changed. Your child still needs unconditional love. They still need to feel like they belong in your family and in the world. They still need boundaries, guidance, and room to make mistakes. They still need time to play, laugh, move, and rest. They still need to know that the people who care for them see them for who they really are.

The tools may look different, but the heart of parenting is the same as it has always been:

(Love + Support + Nurture) x Boundaries = Trust.

A Hopeful—and Realistic—Vision

As you finish this book, we want you to picture what a connected, healthy relationship with your child looks like for your family. It may mean more shared meals, more open conversations about anything and everything, or a weekly ritual that you protect no matter what. It may mean making small but consistent changes—like reclaiming bedtime as a screen-free, quiet connection time. It may mean you start listening to your child with the same curiosity you would offer to a close friend, even when you're tempted to jump in with advice. THIS WILL MEAN PUTTING DOWN YOUR OWN DEVICES!

Remember: meaningful change doesn't require perfection. It requires persistence. You don't need to fix every problem overnight. You don't need to control every influence in your child's life. You can't. But you can control how you show up for them. You can control how you listen, how you respond, and how you model the balance, self-respect, and boundaries you hope they will carry into adulthood.

The goal is not to eliminate every hardship from your child's life. That's impossible—and it's not even desirable. Your goal is to help them become strong enough, and secure enough, to face those hardships with confidence and to know they can always come to you for support.

Your Reason to Be Hopeful

Every time you choose connection over control, listening over lecturing, curiosity over criticism, you are building the kind of relationship that can protect your child's mental health. Every moment you spend understanding their perspective is an investment in trust. Every honest, open conversation plants a seed for future resilience.

The world will continue to change in ways we can't predict. New platforms will replace old ones. Trends will come and go. But the fundamentals will remain: children who feel connected to their parents are better equipped to navigate life's storms.

So, yes, these are challenging times to be a parent. But they are also times of opportunity. You now have the knowledge, the tools, and the awareness to parent with intention—to not just react to the world as it is but to proactively create the home environment your child needs.

If you remember nothing else from this book, remember this: your child doesn't need you to be perfect. They need you to be present, to be curious, to be consistent, and to be willing to grow alongside them. **That is your reason to be hopeful.**

You can do this. You've already started by reading these pages, by asking the hard questions, and by being open to learning new ways of connecting. The fact that you are here—thinking, reflecting, and preparing—tells us that you have what it takes to give your child the best possible foundation.

So go ahead: put down this book and go talk to your child. Ask them something that invites a real answer. Tell them something you appreciate about them. Laugh together. Remind them that no matter what the world throws at them, they have you.

That connection—your connection—is the most powerful antidote to anxiety and depression that your child will ever have. And that is something worth feeling hopeful about.

So, go ahead: **ReConnect.**

Personality Type Resources

To learn more about personality type, we recommend the following books, co-authored by Paul D. Tieger, and other resources:

Nurture by Nature – Understand Your Child's Personality Type – And Become a Better Parent, Tieger and Barron, Little Brown & Company

Do What You Are – Discover the Perfect Career For You Through the Secrets of Personality Type, Tieger and Barron, Little Brown & Company

The Art of SpeedReading People – How to Size People Up and Speak Their Language, Tieger and Barron, Little Brown & Company

Just Your Type – Create the Relationship You've Always Wanted Using the Secrets of Personality Type, Tieger and Barron, Little Brown & Company

Truity.com – Offers a variety of different personality tests and interesting research findings.

Personality Type Glossary

The Jung/Myers Model of Personality Type: The most widely used personality typing system in the world. Four dichotomous "dimensions" identify sixteen discreet personality types that describe how people are energized, what kind of information they naturally notice and remember, how they make decisions, and how they like to organize the world around them.

The Myers-Briggs Type Indicator (MBTI): The psychometric assessment developed by Isabel Myers and Katherine Briggs, published by The Myers & Briggs Company.

Temperament: A theory of personality popularized by psychologist David Keirsey, originally postulated in 450 BCE by Socrates, embraced throughout history by philosophers, writers, and psychologists. It describes four different "human natures" that influence a person's values and key motivators. The names assigned to the temperaments by Paul Tieger in his books are Traditionalists (SJs), Experiencers (SPs), Conceptualizers (NTs), and Idealists (NFs).

Personality Type "preferences"

Extraverts – outwardly focused; energized by being with others

Introverts – inwardly focused; energized by reflecting alone

Sensors – naturally notice and remember concrete details

Intuitive – naturally see patterns and how things are related to one another

Thinkers – tend to make decisions logically and impersonally

Feelers – tend to make decisions based on their and others' values and feelings

Judgers – seek closure; tend to be organized and decisive

Perceivers – seek openness; prefer to be spontaneous and to keep their options open

Introverted-Feeling – process feelings internally; share feelings selectively

Extraverted-Feeling – usually comfortable sharing their feelings with others

Notes

Chapter 3 Personality Types: Why We Are Who We Are

1. The Myers-Briggs Company – Publisher of the Myers-Briggs type Indicator

2. The Jung/Myers Model of Personality Types – as a Way to Identify individuals Most Prone to Anxiety and Depression" / n = 10,500 / Conducted with the University of Minnesota College of Pharmacy, 2019 / The Journal of Behavioral Health Services and Research. This first-of-its-kind study showed a strong correlation between individuals' inborn personality type and predisposition for anxiety and depression. Use of the Jung/Myers Model of Personality Types to Identify and Engage with Individuals at Greatest Risk of Experiencing Depression and Anxiety (springer.com)

3. Validation of the TPI-C (Tieger Personality Indicator for Children) – Sample = proportional representation of child's age, gender, and personality types and parents' race and educational level. 93% of parents indicated their child's type results were "extremely" or "quite" accurate.

Responsible Hard Workers (Type 1). In the MBTI system, people who share this type are called Sensing-Judgers (SJs) and are often described as dependable, organized, productive, service-oriented, trustworthy, traditional, and consistent.

Strategic Problem Solvers (Type 2). In the MBTI system, people who share this type are called Intuitive-Thinkers (NTs) and are often described as competent, confident, independent, intellectual, high achieving, and strategic.

Adventurous Free Spirits (Type 3). In the MBTI system, people who share this type are called Sensing-Thinking Perceivers (STPs) and are often described as fun-loving, risk-taking, spontaneous, active, adaptable, and impulsive.

Gentle Humble Helpers (Type 4). In the MBTI system, people who share this type are called Sensing-Feeling Perceivers (SFPs) and are often described as caring, kind, nurturing, spontaneous, and adaptable.

Creative Sensitive Souls (Type 5). In the MBTI system, people who share this type are called Intuitive-Feelers (NFs) and are often described as empathetic, idealistic, perceptive, creative, spiritual, compassionate, and collaborative.

Technology and Addiction Glossary

Withdrawal: Short-term physical or emotional discomfort after cutting back or stopping (irritability, restlessness, low mood, poor sleep) that improves with time and support.

Variable Ratio Reinforcement: An unpredictable reward schedule (likes, loot boxes, random wins) that strongly reinforces checking and can foster compulsive use.

Urge Surfing: A mindfulness technique: observe an urge like a wave—breathing, noticing sensations—until it naturally subsides without acting on it.

Tolerance: Needing more time, novelty, or intensity (e.g., endless scroll, faster reward cycles) to achieve the same level of relief or excitement.

Sleep Hygiene: Daily habits that promote restorative sleep (regular schedules, low evening light, device curfews, cool/dark rooms) and counteract screen-related insomnia.

Parental Mediation (Active vs. Restrictive): How caregivers guide kids' media use: active = discussion and coaching; restrictive = rules and limits; often combined with co-use.

Nomophobia: Distress or fear related to being without one's phone or connection (battery, signal, or device) and the perceived loss of safety or identity.

Motivational Interviewing (MI): A collaborative counseling style that strengthens intrinsic motivation for change by exploring ambivalence with empathy and autonomy support.

Harm Reduction: Strategies that reduce negative consequences without requiring immediate abstinence (e.g., app timers, content filters, safer-use plans).

Gaming Disorder (ICD-11) / Internet Gaming Disorder (DSM-5-TR): A persistent gaming pattern with impaired control and significant life disruption; formally recognized in ICD-11 and listed for further study in DSM-5-TR.

Fear of Missing Out (FOMO): Anxiety that others are having rewarding experiences without you, driving repetitive checking and overuse of social platforms.

Eye Movement Desensitization and Reprocessing (EMDR): A trauma-focused therapy using bilateral stimulation to help the brain reprocess distressing memories that may fuel avoidance or addictive coping.

Doomscrolling: Compulsive consumption of negative or alarming online content that elevates anxiety while making it hard to stop.

Digital Detox: A planned, time-limited break from screens or specific apps to reset habits, regain attention, and assess what's genuinely helpful.

Dialectical Behavior Therapy (DBT): A therapy emphasizing mindfulness, distress tolerance, emotion regulation, and interpersonal effectiveness to reduce impulsive, addictive, or self-harming behaviors.

Cue Reactivity (Triggers): The automatic mind–body response (thoughts, feelings, impulses) to people, places, times, or notifications that have been paired with use.

Craving: A strong, often cue-triggered urge to use a device, app, or substance; it typically rises, peaks, and falls if not acted upon.

Cognitive Behavioral Therapy (CBT): A skills-based therapy that helps people notice and change unhelpful thought–behavior loops driving compulsive use, using tools like thought records and behavioral experiments.

Boundaries (Digital): Planned limits on when, where, and how devices or apps are used (e.g., no phones at meals; screens off after 10 pm), plus agreed-upon consequences and support.

Behavioral Addiction: A pattern of compulsive engagement in a rewarding behavior (e.g., gaming, social media) despite harm, marked by loss of control, tolerance, and withdrawal-like symptoms.

Valuable Resources

Global Digital Detox and Technology Addiction Programs

Compiled: September 2025 •
Verify details with providers before referring/enrolling.

This directory of inpatient/residential and outpatient services is focused on technology, internet, social media, and gaming-related addictions. Listings for services in the U.S. appear first, followed by those in other regions.

In the U.S.
1. reSTART Life (Digital Recovery) – Fall City and Bellevue, Washington — Residential, PHP/IOP, Outpatient — Teens and Adults — Specialized treatment for digital overuse, internet/gaming disorder; nature-based residential campus. — https://www.restartlife.com

2. RESET Summer Camp – Santa Barbara, California — 4-week Residential Summer Program — Teens and Young Adults — Clinically designed tech detox program with academic and life skills support. — https://www.resetsummercamp.com/

3. Foothills at Red Oak Recovery – Ellenboro, North Carolina — Residential (for boys 14–17) — Adolescents (boys) — Treats technology and internet addiction alongside substance use and mental health. — https://foothillsatredoakrecovery.com/teen-internet-addiction-treatment/

4. SunCloud Health – Adolescent Program (Process Addictions) — Northbrook, Illinois (Chicagoland) — PHP/IOP, Outpatient — Adolescents — Includes support for social media/technology overuse alongside co-occurring issues. — https://suncloudhealth.com/therapy-programs/adolescents

5. Newport Healthcare (Newport Academy / Newport Institute) – Multiple U.S. locations — Residential, PHP/IOP, Outpatient — Teens (Academy) and Young Adults (Institute) — Addresses screen/social media overuse as part of comprehensive MH/SUD

treatment. — https://www.newportacademy.com/resources/mental-health/screen-time-teen-mental-health/

6. **Embark Behavioral Health (network)** – Multiple U.S. locations — Residential, Day Treatment, IOP, Outpatient — Teens and Young Adults — Treats technology/social media addiction within broader mental-health programs. — https://www.embarkbh.com/conditions/technology-addiction/

7. **Midwest Institute for Addiction** – Video Game and Technology Disorders — St. Louis and Kansas City, Missouri — Outpatient — Adolescents and Adults — Outpatient therapy for video game and technology-related disorders. — https://www.midwestinstituteforaddiction.org/video-game-technology-disorders/

8. **J. Flowers Health Institute** – Technology Addiction — Houston, Texas — Comprehensive Diagnostic and Evaluation, Outpatient — Adolescents and Adults — Concierge-style diagnostics and treatment plans for technology addiction and co-occurring conditions. — https://jflowershealth.com/technology-addiction/

9. **Omega Recovery** – Technology and Gaming Program — Austin, Texas — Residential, PHP/IOP, Outpatient — Adults (18+) — Adventure and evidence-based care tracks for technology/gaming addiction. — https://www.omegarecovery.org/treatment/technology-addiction/

10. **Massachusetts General Hospital** – Digital Addiction and Gambling Program (ARMS) — Boston, Massachusetts — Outpatient (CBT, family therapy) — Teens and Young Adults — Specialized clinic addressing problematic technology use and gambling; referral-based. — https://www.massgeneral.org/psychiatry/treatments-and-services/digital-addiction-and-gambling-treatment-program

---

Outside the U.S,

India:
NIMHANS – SHUT Clinic (Service for Healthy Use of Technology) — Bengaluru, Karnataka — Outpatient; Parent groups; Community programs — Adolescents and Adults — India's first

tech-de-addiction clinic; clinical services and public programs for problematic technology use. — https://www.nimhans.ac.in/

Thailand:
The Edge (The Cabin Group) – Gaming and Internet Misuse — Chiang Mai, Thailand — Residential (young men 18–26, case-by-case older) — Young Men — Adventure-based residential program; treats misuse of internet and gaming. — https://www.theedgerehab.com/

Singapore:
National Addictions Management Service (NAMS) – Institute of Mental Health, Singapore — Inpatient Detox; Outpatient; Support Groups — Adolescents and Adults — National service treating behavioral addictions including internet/gaming; parent groups available. — https://www.nams.sg/

Canada:
Last Door Recovery Society – Media and Video Game Addiction Group — New Westminster, British Columbia — Outpatient Group Program — Adults — Twelve-week group focusing on media/internet/gaming as process addictions. — https://lastdoor.org/addiction-treatment/video-game-addiction-treatment-and-media-addiction-treatment/

Canada:
Trafalgar Addiction Treatment Centre – Gaming Addiction — Ontario (GTA) — Inpatient and Outpatient — Adults — Dedicated video-game addiction treatment with virtual options. — https://trafalgarresidence.com/gaming-addiction-treatment/

Canada:
CAMH – Problem Gambling and Technology Use Service – Toronto, Ontario — Outpatient Groups and Therapy — Youth (16–25), Adults, Families — Specialized groups for problematic technology use (gaming, internet, social media). — https://www.camh.ca/en/patients-and-families/programs-and-services/problem-gambling--technology-use-treatment

UK:
Nightingale Hospital – Technology Addiction — London, England — Inpatient and Outpatient — Adults — Private mental health hospital with specialist technology addiction therapists. — https://www.nightingalehospital.co.uk/technology-addiction/

UK:
Delamere — Digital/Internet and Social Media Addiction — Cheshire, England — Residential Rehab — Adults — Purpose-built private rehab with digital addiction treatment pathway. — https://delamere.com/addiction-treatment/behavioural/internet-social-media

UK:
Priory Group – Internet Addiction Treatment — Multiple locations across UK — Inpatient, Outpatient, Online — Adults (some adolescent services) — Network offering therapy and rehab for internet and technology addiction. — https://www.priorygroup.com/addiction-treatment/internet-addiction-treatment

UK:
National Centre for Gaming Disorders (NHS – CNWL) – London, England — Outpatient (NHS clinic) — Ages 13+ — National NHS clinic dedicated to gaming disorder; family-inclusive care. — https://www.cnwl.nhs.uk/national-centre-gaming-disorders

---

Fellowships and Communities

The following information lists major global fellowships and self-help communities relevant to technology/screen use, gaming, pornography/sex, and online shopping/overspending.

It is included for informational purposes and not meant to be an endorsement. Programs, ages, and levels of care change, so you should confirm directly with each provider.

Global 12-Step and Self-Help Programs for: Technology/Screen, Gaming, Porn/Sex, and Shopping Addictions
Compiled September 2025

Game Quitters: Video game overuse — Peer self-help community and education — Global; online — https://gamequitters.com/

NoFap: Porn overuse/compulsive sexual behavior — Peer self-help community — Global; online — https://nofap.com/

Spenders Anonymous (S.A.): Compulsive spending/shopping — 12-Step fellowship — Global; online — https://www.spenders.org/

Debtors Anonymous (DA): Compulsive debt/overspending, including online shopping — 12-Step fellowship — Global; online and in-person — https://debtorsanonymous.org/

Sex Addicts Anonymous (SAA): Sexual addiction (including compulsive porn use) — 12-Step fellowship — Global; online and in-person — https://saa-recovery.org/

Online Gamers Anonymous (OLGA / OLG-Anon): Gaming addiction; family and loved ones — 12-Step-inspired self-help — Online — https://olganon.org/

Gaming Addicts Anonymous (GAA): Video game addiction — 12-Step fellowship — Global; online and in-person — https://www.gamingaddictsanonymous.org/

Media Addicts Anonymous (MAA): Media/tech overuse (social, streaming, gaming, shopping, porn, news) — 12-Step fellowship — Global; daily online; some in-person — https://www.mediaaddictsanonymous.org/

Internet and Technology Addicts Anonymous (ITAA): Internet and technology overuse (social media, phone, streaming, gaming, porn, shopping, info) — 12-Step fellowship — Global; online and in-person — https://internetaddictsanonymous.org/

Recommended Books about:
Technology, Screen/Gaming, Porn/Sex, and Shopping Addictions
Compiled September 2025

These widely read titles cover technology overuse, attention, gaming, pornography/sex, and shopping addictions. Links go to the publisher or official pages where possible.

1: The Anxious Generation – Jonathan Haidt — Phones and social media/youth mental health — https://www.penguinrandomhouse.com/books/729231/the-anxious-generation-by-jonathan-haidt/

2. Technology Addiction: A guide to recognize and deal with technology dependence in our lives – Michael Shelby - https://www.planbecounseling.com/

3: To Buy or Not to Buy – April Lane Benson, PhD — Shopping/overspending compulsion — https://www.penguinrandomhouse.com/books/11549/to-buy-or-not-to-buy-by-april-lane-benson/

4: Out of the Shadows – Patrick J. Carnes, PhD — Sex addiction (foundational text) — https://www.hazelden.org/store/item/2192?Out-of-the-Shadows-Third-Edition=

5: Your Brain on Porn – Gary Wilson — Pornography addiction (lay guide) — https://www.amazon.com/Your-Brain-Porn-Pornography-Addiction/dp/099316160X

6: Reset Your Child's Brain – Victoria L. Dunckley, MD — Four-week plan for screen-time related issues — https://newworldlibrary.com/product/reset-your-child's-brain

7: Dopamine Nation – Anna Lembke, MD — Addiction and high-dopamine behaviors (including tech/porn/shopping) — https://www.penguinrandomhouse.com/books/624957/dopamine-nation-by-anna-lembke-md/

8: Stolen Focus – Johann Hari — Attention crisis (screens & modern life)—https://www.penguinrandomhouse.com/books/634289/stolen-focus-by-johann-hari/

9: Glow Kids – Nicholas Kardaras — Screen addiction in children & teens — https://us.macmillan.com/books/9781250146557/glowkids/

10: Irresistible – Adam Alter — Behavioral addiction & rsuasive tech — https://www.penguinrandomhouse.com/books/318516/irresistible-by-adam-alter/

11: Digital Minimalism — Cal Newport — Technology overuse & intentional reduction — https://www.penguinrandomhouse.com/books/575667/digital-minimalism-by-cal-newport/

Appendix

Additional Data
Compiled: September 2025

Mental Illness Among College Students

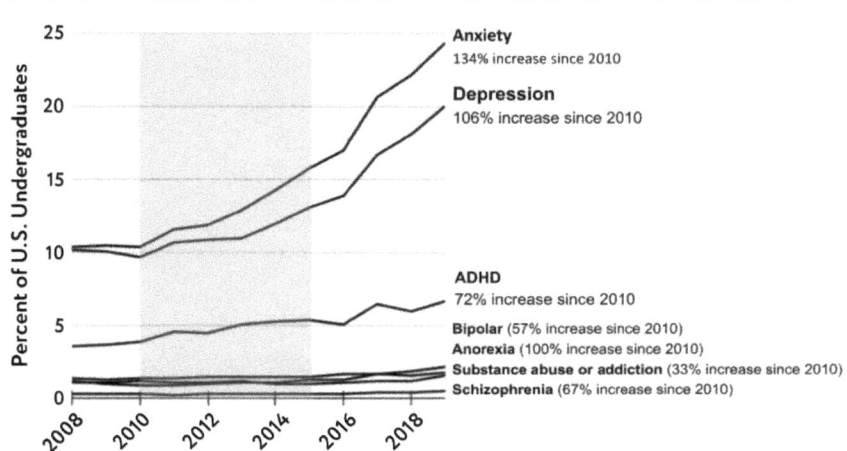

Figure 1.2. Percent of U.S. undergraduates with each of several mental illnesses. Rates of diagnosis of various mental illnesses increased in the 2010s among college students, especially for anxiety and depression. (Source: American College Health Association.)[9]

Anxiety Prevalence by Age

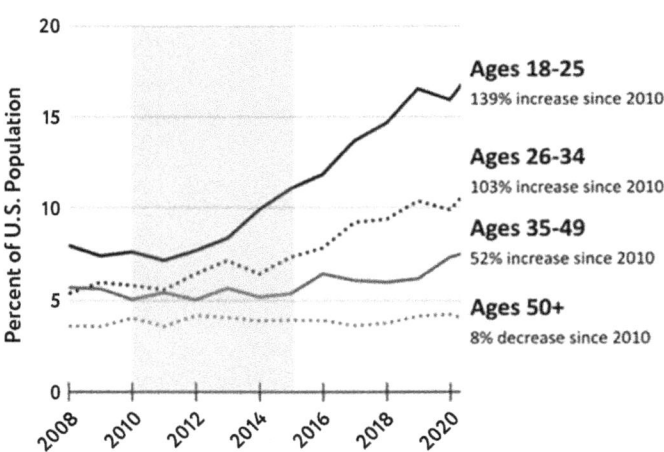

Figure 1.3. Percent of U.S. adults reporting high levels of anxiety by age group. (Source: U.S. National Survey on Drug Use and Health.)[11]

Emergency Room Visits for Self-Harm

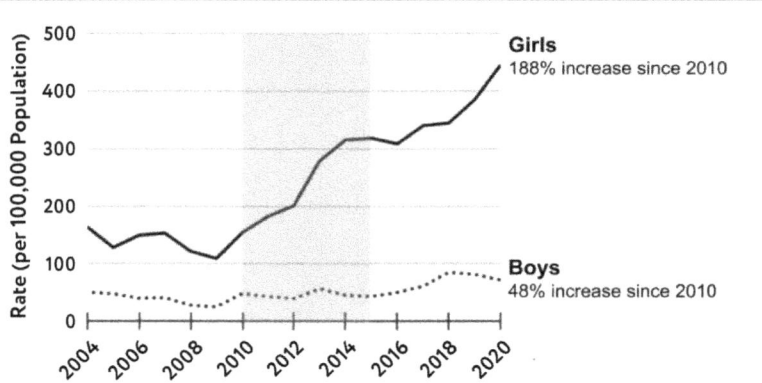

Figure 1.4. The rate per 100,000 in the U.S. population at which adolescents (ages 10–14) are treated in hospital emergency rooms for nonfatal self-injury. (Source: U.S. Centers for Disease Control, National Center for Injury Prevention and Control.)[20]

Communication Technology Adoption

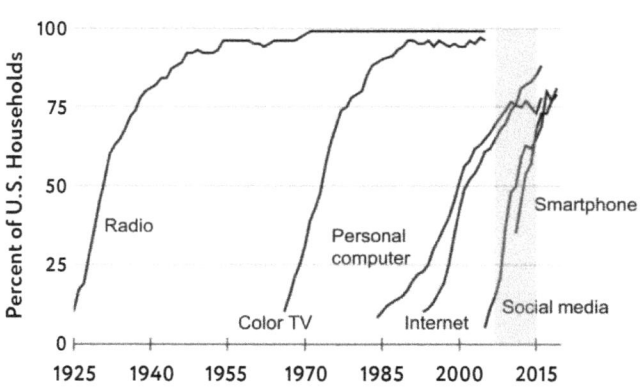

Figure 1.6. The share of U.S. households using specific technologies. The smartphone was adopted faster than any other communication technology in history. (Source: Our World in Data.)[25]

Have a Few Close Friends

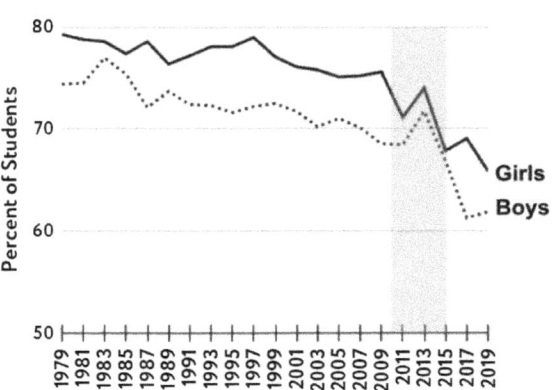

Meet Up with Friends Daily

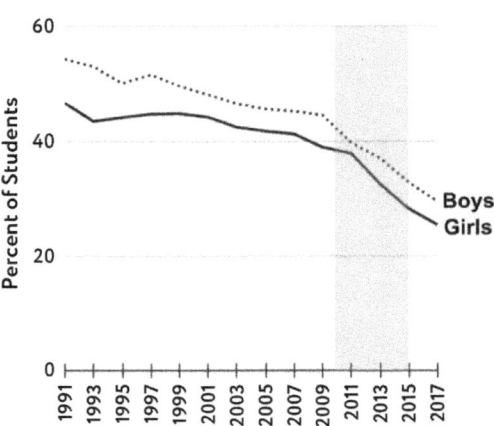

Figure 2.1. Percentage of U.S. students (8th, 10th, and 12th grade) who say that they meet up with their friends "almost every day" outside school.[12] (Source: Monitoring the Future. I explain how I use this important dataset in the endnotes.)[13]

Daily Time with Friends, by Age Group

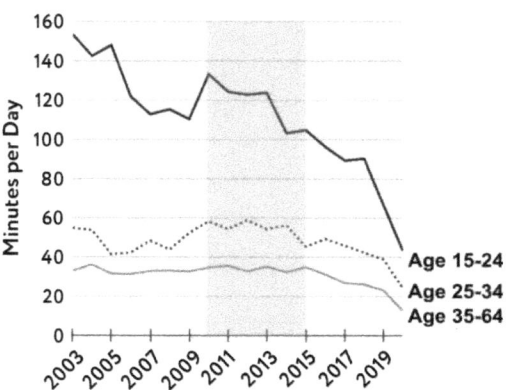

Figure 5.1. Daily average time spent with friends in minutes. Only the youngest age group shows a sharp drop before the 2020 data collection, which was performed after COVID restrictions had begun. (Source: American Time Use Study.)[19]

Satisfied with Oneself

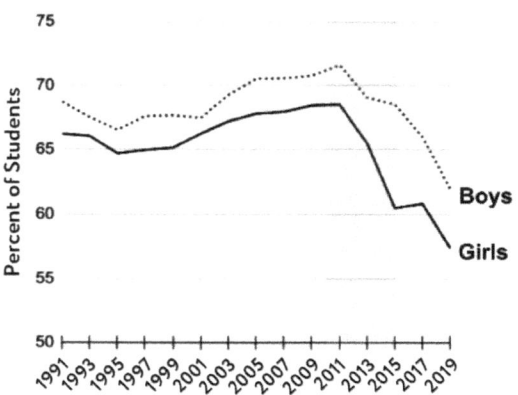

Figure 6.5. The sociometer plunge of 2012. Percent of U.S. students (8th, 10th, and 12th grade) who said they were satisfied with themselves. (Source: Monitoring the Future.)

No Chance of a Successful Life

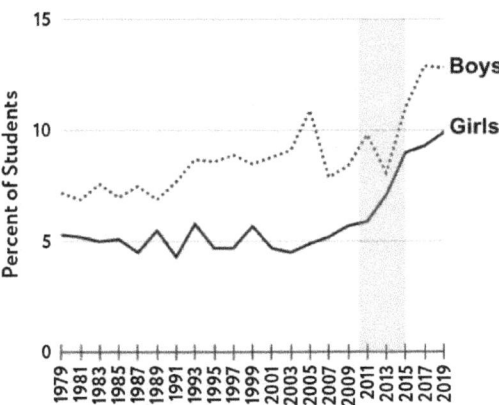

Figure 7.1. Percent of U.S. high school seniors who agreed or mostly agreed with the statement "People like me don't have much of a chance at a successful life." (Source: Monitoring the Future.)[2]

Life Often Feels Meaningless

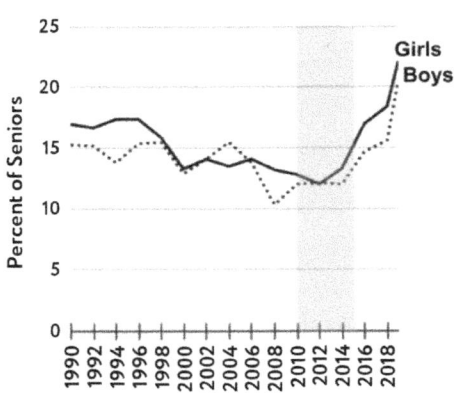

Figure 7.6. Percent of U.S. high school seniors who agreed or mostly agreed with the statement "Life often feels meaningless." (Source: Monitoring the Future.)

www.ingramcontent.com/pod-product-compliance
Lightning Source LLC
Chambersburg PA
CBHW052128030426
42337CB00028B/5067